Veterinary Notes for
DOG
BREEDERS

For the dog breeder there are many ways to measure success. Achievement in the show ring is one of the most important endorsements of the breeder's efforts. Here the homebred Dandie Dinmont Terrier Ch. Abington's Wingate's Fancy is presented with the Best in Show award at the Boardwalk KC show under judge Gayle Bontecou. "Annie" was shown to this good win by Peggy Ozorowski for owners Lois Weiner and Laura Green. *John Ashbey*

Veterinary Notes for

DOG BREEDERS

Annette M. Carricato, V.M.D.

HOWELL BOOK HOUSE

New York

Maxwell Macmillan Canada
Toronto

Maxwell Macmillan International
New York   Oxford   Singapore   Sydney

Howell Book House
Macmillan Publishing Company
866 Third Avenue
New York, NY 10022

Maxwell Macmillan Canada, Inc.
1200 Eglinton Avenue East, Suite 200
Don Mills, Ontario M3C 3N1

Macmillan Publishing Company is part of the Maxwell Communication Group of Companies.

Library of Congress Cataloging-in-Publication Data

Carricato, Annette M.
Veterinary notes for dog breeders / by Annette M. Carricato.
p. cm.
Includes bibliographical references.
ISBN 0-87605-805-5
1. Dogs—Breeding. 2. Dogs—Diseases. 3. Dogs—Reproduction.
4. Kennel management. I. Title.
SF427.2C37 1992
636.7′08′2—dc20   91-19288

Macmillan books are available at special discounts for bulk purchases for sales promotions, premiums, fund-raising, or educational use. For details, contact:

Special Sales Director
Macmillan Publishing Company
866 Third Avenue
New York, NY 10022

10 9 8 7 6 5 4 3 2 1

Printed in the United States of America

Contents

Foreword

BY ANY OBJECTIVE STANDARD, dog breeding is an ideal example of applied science combined with enlightened husbandry, much of which comes to us through veterinary research, enabling us to produce quality dogs and provide them with an environment not possible in decades past.

When a breeder brings about a mating between a dog and bitch, he or she triggers a dramatic series of amazing phenomena that culminates in the birth of a litter some sixty-three days later. By the breeder's agency, all the natural laws governing the development of new organisms are activated whether we understand them or not.

As we increase our knowledge of biology, heredity and other related sciences, we apply what we learn to achieve these objectives. Yet, just as there will never be a perfect dog, there will never be a perfect dog-keeping environment. There will always be more to learn, understand and achieve in the quest for the dog of our dreams and the way we care for it.

Veterinary Notes for Dog Breeders is both bridge and tool to use in connection with that quest. It is a bridge between the veterinarian who has the knowledge and the breeder who seeks the benefit of this knowledge to refine a breeding program and the husbandry skills needed to care for fine animals. It is a tool that enables the breeder to use what appears in these pages to achieve the goals he or she is attempting to reach.

Modern breeders have a vast body of scientific information available to them as never before. *Veterinary Notes for Dog Breeders* mirrors this happy state with wide-ranging coverage of numerous topics all serious dog breeders must be familiar with to operate effectively.

That this book answers the needs of the intended audience is a given. What is very special about *Veterinary Notes for Dog Breeders* is the fact that the veterinary authority who speaks to the fancy in these pages is one of the fancy's own. This simple fact gives new meaning to the term "user friendly" where this outstanding book is concerned.

Dr. Carricato is a graduate of the University of Pennsylvania, a practicing veterinarian and a successful breeder-exhibitor of English Setters. She is keenly aware of what will best serve the serious breeder in a reference of this kind. To Dr. Carricato's credit, *Veterinary Notes for Dog Breeders* does merit its place in every serious breeder's library. We, in turn, feel privileged to have a hand in bringing it to you.

THE PUBLISHER

Veterinary Notes for DOG BREEDERS

PART ONE

Screening for Genetic Diseases

THE OBJECTIVE OF SCREENING for genetic diseases is ultimately to breed healthy dogs. Breeding healthy dogs, however, is not a simple task. It requires a lot of effort on your part. As a breeder, you must be dedicated enough to study a myriad of genetic diseases. This section was written to provide you with information about a number of genetic diseases that may confront you. This base of knowledge is the science behind dog breeding. You must also take an objective look at available breeding stock and make some difficult decisions regarding which dogs to breed and which not to breed. No one can make those difficult decisions for you. Decision making is the art (and the fun) behind dog breeding. Now for the work.

The English Setter Ch. Kadon's Shooting Star, owned by the author and bred by Kay Monaghan, was examined by OFA at twenty-six months, and the certification of the dog's hip joint conformation appears below.

ORTHOPEDIC FOUNDATION FOR ANIMALS INC.

KADONS SHOOTING STAR, CH.
registered name of dog

ENGLISH SETTER
breed

BLUE BELTON
color

177506838
tattoo

314191
Application Number

SEPTEMBER 18, 1989
Date of Report

SF-049184
registration no. (AKC, CKC)

MALE
sex

MAY   20, 1987
date of birth

26
Age at evaluation in months

ES-2454G26M-T
O.F.A. REGISTRY NUMBER

This registry number issued with the right to correct or revoke by the Orthopedic Foundation for Animals.

BASED UPON THE RADIOGRAPH SUBMITTED THE CONSENSUS WAS THAT NO EVIDENCE OF HIP DYSPLASIA WAS RECOGNIZED.

THE HIP JOINT CONFORMATION WAS EVALUATED AS: GOOD

owner

ANNETTE CARRICATO, VMD
3740 DERRY ST
HARRISBURG, PA 17111

E. A. Corley

E. A. CORLEY, D.V.M.
PROJECT DIRECTOR

DYSPLASIA CONTROL REGISTRY

5744

1

The Orthopedic
Foundation for Animals

THE ORTHOPEDIC FOUNDATION for Animals (OFA) is a nonprofit organization assisted by board-certified veterinary radiologists. The purpose of the OFA is to evaluate potential breeding animals for the presence or absence of orthopedic diseases that can be genetically transmitted. Breeders most often use the OFA to certify their dogs as being free of hip or elbow dysplasia. The OFA can also be used to detect many other orthopedic diseases. Please write to the OFA, talk to your veterinarian or refer to *Medical and Genetic Aspects of Purebred Dogs* for information on which orthopedic diseases your breed may be prone to develop. Each national breed club is entitled to have a representative to the OFA. If your breed club doesn't have one, find out why. Representatives periodically receive information from the OFA for dissemination to club members. If your breed club has a representative but you are not receiving any information, find out why not.

HIP DYSPLASIA

The OFA will evaluate hip films of young dogs but will not issue breed numbers until the dogs are at least two years old. Preliminary films of dogs less than two years old are read by only one radiologist. The resultant report issued is called a Preliminary (Consultation) Report.

Films of dogs older than two are read by three different radiologists. The resultant report is issued is a consensus opinion of these three radiologists. Seven different consensus opinions are possible. Hips cleared by the OFA are considered to be excellent, good or fair and are given a breed number. Hips failed by the OFA are considered to be mildly, moderately or severely dysplastic and are not granted breed numbers. Some hips are not given final consensus opinions; in such cases, the hips must be reevaluated in six to eight months.

OFA breed numbers are coded to provide information at a glance. Let's take as an example the OFA number ES2454G26M-T. "ES" is the OFA's abbreviation for the English Setter breed. This dog is the 2,454th English Setter to be given a number. "G" stands for a rating of good. (If a rating of fair is given, "F" is used; if a rating of excellent is given, "E" is used.) This dog was twenty-six months old when evaluated. The "M" stands for male. ("F" is used for females.) A "T" is placed at the end of the OFA number if the dog has a tattoo at the time of evaluation.

Ratings are given because hip dysplasia is not an all-or-none phenomenon. Think of dysplasia as a continuum, much as eye pigment is a continuum. A dark-eyed dog is obvious; likewise, a light-eyed dog is obvious. But in between are a lot of dogs that have eyes that are "relatively" dark or "somewhat" light. Many people become frustrated with the OFA because bitches rated fair by the OFA bred to dogs rated fair by the OFA can produce entirely dysplastic litters. Is anyone surprised to find light-eyed litters when "somewhat" light-eyed dogs are bred to "somewhat" light-eyed dogs?

The OFA recommends that you breed only dogs that are as good as or better than average if you hope to minimize the frequency of dysplasia in your lines. Please note that according to OFA definitions, an OFA rating of fair is below average for the breed. In other words, the OFA recommends that you use only dogs that have a rating of good or excellent.

Application for Radiographic Evaluation

Please Type or Print Legibly

Orthopedic Foundation for Animals, Inc.
2300 Nifong Blvd.
Columbia, MO 65201

Tel. (314) 442-0418

previous application no. if any

registered name of dog	registration no. — AKC - CKC - other
breed	sex
color	date of birth
tattoo, if any	date radiograph taken — film no.
owner's name — co-owner	veterinarian's name or veterinary hospital
mailing address	mailing address
city — state — zip	city — state — zip
telephone number ( )	telephone number ( )

I hereby certify that the radiograph submitted is of the dog described on this card. I am aware that the radiograph will be retained for the records of the Orthopedic Foundation for Animals, Inc., and I authorize the OFA to release the OFA number, which includes the phenotypic evaluation, to the A.K.C., applicable breed club and referring veterinarian.

Signature of owner or authorized representative _____

(OVER)

The Dysplasia Control Registry of the OFA is a voluntary program established to evaluate radiographs of purebred dogs and to identify films showing no radiographic evidence of canine hip dysplasia or other orthopedic problems. All films submitted that are of acceptable diagnostic quality will be reviewed by a panel of qualified veterinary radiologists and a consensus report will be returned to the owner of record and referring veterinarian. Only dogs that are 24 months of age or older at the time of radiography, with no radiographic evidence of hip dysplasia, will be assigned a breed OFA number. The OFA does offer a consultation service for dogs under 24 months of age.

VETERINARY INFORMATION

This dog was restrained using:
1. Physical Restraint only _____
2. Chemical Restraint
   Anesthesia _____ type _____
   Tranquilizer _____ type _____
   Other _____ type _____

Veterinarians signature _____

Front and back of a sample OFA application form. Reprinted with permission.

INSTRUCTIONS

Radiographs should be permanently identified in the film emulsion with:

1. Registered name and/or number of the dog
2. Name of veterinarian or hospital making the film
3. Date radiograph taken
4. Breed & date of birth,

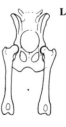

R   L

Pelvic evaluations are based upon the standard VD view as illustrated.

Good pelvic definition. Pelvis not tilted, Femurs extended and parallel.

Fee Schedule:
Hip Dysplasia Registry (dogs over 24 months of age)—$20.00
Hips plus elbows—$25.00
Preliminary hip evaluation (dogs under 24 months of age)—$15.00
Other radiographic consultations—$15.00

Orthopedic Foundation for Animals
Preliminary (Consultation) Report

registered name of dog	registration no. (AKC, CKC)
breed	sex
color	Date of Birth
tattoo	Age at evaluation in months
Application number	Date of Report

owner

veterinarian

RADIOGRAPHIC EVALUATION OF PELVIC PHENOTYPE WITH RESPECT TO CANINE HIP DYSPLASIA

The study must be repeated when the dog is 24 months of age or older to qualify for an OFA Breed Registry Number.

_____ **EXCELLENT HIP JOINT CONFORMATION***
superior hip joint conformation as compared with other individuals of the same breed and age

_____ **GOOD HIP JOINT CONFORMATION***
well formed hip joint conformation as compared with other individuals of the same breed and age.

_____ **FAIR HIP JOINT CONFORMATION***
minor irregularities of hip joint conformation as compared with other individuals of the same breed and age

_____ **BORDERLINE HIP JOINT CONFORMATION**
marginal hip joint conformation of indeterminate status with respect to hip dysplasia at this time

_____ **MILD HIP DYSPLASIA**
radiographic evidence of minor dysplastic change of the hip joints

_____ **MODERATE HIP DYSPLASIA**
well defined radiographic evidence of dysplastic changes of the hip joints

_____ **SEVERE HIP DYSPLASIA**
radiographic evidence of marked dysplastic changes of the hip joints

RADIOGRAPHIC FINDINGS

HIP JOINTS - STANDARD VD VIEW

_____ subluxation
_____ remodeling of femoral head/neck
_____ osteoarthritis/degenerative joint disease
_____ shallow acetabula
_____ acetabular rim/edge change
_____ unilateral pathology

ELBOW JOINTS - FLEXED LATERAL VIEW

_____ negative for elbow dysplasia ___ L ___ R
_____ ununited anconeal process ___ L ___ R
_____ osteoarthritis degenerative joint disease

MISCELLANEOUS

_____ previous fracture
_____ soft tissue calcification
_____ foreign body
_____ _____

Consultation by: _E. A. Corley, DVM_

Sample OFA Preliminary (Consultation) Report. Reprinted with permission.

6

Some dogs have unilateral hip dysplasia; that is, only one hip is dysplastic. This seems to be a familial trait and usually involves the same hip in affected relatives.

Hip dysplasia is a developmental disease. Puppies are not born dysplastic; rather, they develop dysplasia over time. Some dogs are so severely affected that the disease is radiographically obvious at six months of age. Other dogs are more mildly affected, and radiographic evidence is not obvious until they are much older. The vast majority of dysplastic dogs will show radiographic evidence of disease by two years of age. This is why the OFA will not issue a breed number to dogs less than two years of age.

Hip dysplasia is a radiographic diagnosis; that is, it can be definitely diagnosed only with the use of X-rays. The key radiographic sign of early hip dysplasia is subluxation. Subluxation simply means that the hip joint is not seated deeply enough. With time, subluxation leads to secondary changes in the joint that are much more obvious on a radiograph. These secondary changes are due to the development of arthritis within the affected hip joint.

If you take the time to learn some basic radiographic anatomy, you will see more when you look at radiographs. There are two components of a hip joint—the femur, or thighbone, and the pelvic acetabulum, or cup. The important parts of the femur are the neck, the head and the physeal scar. The neck joins the bulk of the thigh bone with the femoral head. The head is much more obvious if the physeal scar is envisioned as the ball portion of the ball-and-socket joint. The socket portion of the joint is the cup-shaped acetabulum. The acetabulum is much easier to envision by remembering that the cup is three-dimensional. The dorsal and cranial rims form the roof and side edges of the socket respectively; there is no floor.

Subluxated hips are characterized by shallow acetabula and irregular joint margins. Normal joints have femoral heads that are deeply seated in cup-shaped acetabula and have smooth, regularly shaped joint margins.

Severely dysplastic hips show secondary signs of arthritis. The femoral heads are remodeled and flattened and the necks are thickened.

Radiographs should not be interpreted if they are not the best quality obtainable. They should have both good detail and good positioning. Essential details may be obscured if the machine is incorrectly set. If the dog is not positioned well, interpretation is meaningless. Good positioning requires that the dog be symmetrical.

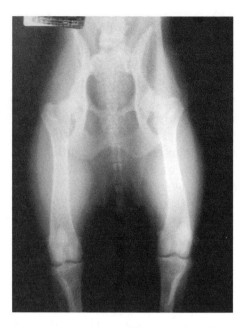

Radiograph of a symmetrically positioned pelvis.

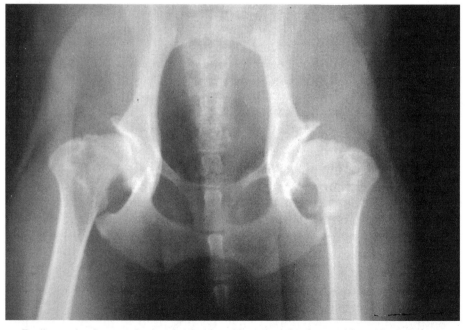

Radiograph of severely dysplastic hips. Note that the femoral head is flattened, the neck is thickened and the acetabulae are very shallow and irregularly shaped.

If the pelvis is tilted, one hip will appear to be more deeply seated than it really is and the other hip will appear to be more shallow than it really is. If the pelvis is positioned symmetrically, the right fossa will be the same size as the left. Good positioning also requires that the legs be parallel to one another, turned inward. If the legs are positioned correctly, the kneecaps will be centered over the far ends of the femurs.

Controversy currently exists regarding the use of anesthesia in order to obtain OFA hip films. Please note that the back of the application form now has a blank section regarding restraint. At the present time, restraint may be either physical or chemical. Chemical restraint may range from mild tranquilization to general anesthesia. A controversial study was published that showed that high-quality radiographs could be taken without resorting to chemical restraint. The problem with this study is that it did not compare the *diagnostic* quality of these radiographs with radiographs taken using anesthesia. The study showed that X-rays could be obtained of dogs that were positioned well without the use of general anesthesia, but it did not show whether these X-rays were as good in showing subtle signs of subluxation as those taken using general anethesia.

Many breeders believe that films taken under anesthesia may provide a false diagnosis of hip dysplasia. They believe that the anesthesia relaxes the joint and allows for subluxation that is not normally present. Most veterinarians disagree. They believe that dogs that appear to be subluxated under anesthesia are truly dysplastic. There are two conditions, however, that do seem to cause subluxation to appear on radiographs of dogs that are not truly dysplastic. One of these conditions is estrus. The other is prolonged inactivity.

Dogs determined to be mildy affected may be treated with exercise restriction and pain medications. Severely affected dogs should be treated surgically. Three surgical procedures are currently available to treat dogs with hip dysplasia. Young puppies with signs of severe dysplasia may be treated with a surgery known as a triple pelvic osteotomy. The surgical procedure re-forms the hip joint so that the femur is seated more deeply in the acetabulum. It is only useful if performed before degenerative arthritis has destroyed the joint. Adult dogs with severe arthritis may be treated surgically with either a femoral head and neck excision or a total hip replacement. When the femoral head is excised, or removed, the dog's source of pain is also removed. Surrounding leg muscles must be able to support the weight of the hind leg. Therefore, most surgeons decline performing the surgery on large dogs. Total hip replacement is self-explanatory. It alleviates pain and provides useful function of the hind legs. However, the surgery is expensive. Any surgery performed for hip dysplasia must be done one leg at a time. This will allow treated dogs to have one functional leg to use while recovering from surgery on the opposite leg.

Many different breeds are afflicted with hip dysplasia. Refer to the OFA, your veterinarian or *Medical and Genetic Aspects of Purebred Dogs* if you do not know whether hip dysplasia is a concern for your particular breed. The current address for the OFA is 2300 Nifong Boulevard, Columbia, MO 65201.

ELBOW DYSPLASIA

Hip dysplasia and elbow dysplasia have many similarities. Elbow dysplasia is also a developmental disease that eventually results in arthritic joint changes within the elbow joint.

Elbow dysplasia may be caused by any one of three different developmental defects. The three defects are ununited anconeal process (UAP), fragmented coronoid process (FCP) and osteochondrosis dessicans (OCD). OCD will be discussed in the following section. UAP and FCP are both due to abnormal growth of one of the two points located within the elbow joint. The two points are known as the anconeal and the coronoid processes. These two points have growth plates between them and the rest of the ulnar bone. The growth plates do not fuse properly in affected dogs. Eventually, arthritis develops secondary to the original defect.

Radiographic evidence of arthritis is usually apparent by two years of age. Therefore, the OFA will issue preliminary reports but will not issue breed numbers before the dog reaches twenty-four months of age. Preliminary reports are issued by one radiologist and consensus reports are based on an average of three separate opinions. Normal elbows are not graded. Dysplastic elbows are graded as Grade I (minimal changes), Grade II (moderate changes) and Grade III (severe arthritis). Breed numbers are coded to indicate the breed of dog and the number of that breed that have already been cleared. For example, GS-EL2 indicates that this was the second German Shepherd Dog cleared of elbow dysplasia by the OFA.

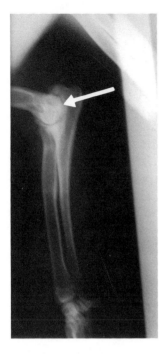

Radiograph showing elbow dysplasia in a German Shepherd Dog. The arrow indicates an ununited anconeal process.

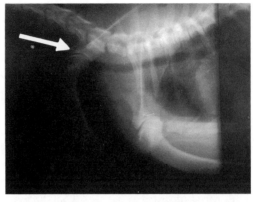

Radiograph of a normal shoulder taken to detect osteochondrosis dessicans (OCD). The arrow points to the shoulder joint.

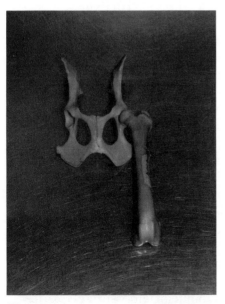

The pelvis bones and left femur illustrating the position used to take hip films.

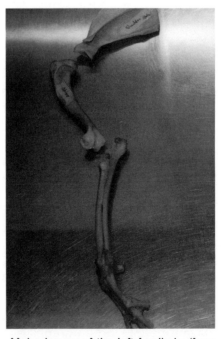

Major bones of the left forelimb: (from top) scapula, humerus, radius, ulna.

Affected dogs usually "wing" or throw out the elbow when gaiting. Lameness is most pronounced after exercise. One or both elbows may be affected. Elbow dysplasia has been reported most frequently in the German Shepherd Dog and the Afghan Hound. In general, large breeds are most often affected. Early surgical removal of any offending points may delay arthritic changes and improve function.

MISCELLANEOUS SKELETAL DISEASES

Many other orthopedic diseases that are suspected of being heritable exist for which there is no breed registry. All these diseases, however, can be diagnosed with appropriate radiographs and should be noted when discovered to be a problem with a particular breed. The most common skeletal diseases recognized that may have a genetic basis include osteochondrosis dessicans, craniomandibular osteopathy, hypertrophic osteodystrophy, eosinophilic panosteitis, wobbler syndrome, atlantoaxial subluxation, Legg-Calve-Perthes' disease and medial patellar luxation. Each disease will be discussed individually in the following sections.

Osteochondrosis Dessicans

Osteochondrosis dessicans, better known as OCD, is believed to be inherited. It affects joint surfaces, most often the shoulder joint. Other joints that may be affected are the knee, the hock and the elbow.

Large-breed male puppies are most likely to develop OCD. Although any large puppy may develop OCD, the following breeds are especially prone to developing OCD: Border Collie, Brittany Spaniel, Golden Retriever, Great Dane and Labrador Retriever.

Affected puppies often begin limping between six and nine months of age. Varying degrees of lameness may be noted, and signs are often intermittent.

Radiographs of diseased joints may reveal irregularities in the cartilage that lines the joint surface. Since OCD is frequently bilateral, both sides of the dog should be radiographed. As with hip dysplasia, properly positioned radiographs are needed to accurately diagnose OCD. Radiographs of the shoulder are most likely to reveal OCD if the joint is positioned over the windpipe. Several views

Orthopedic Foundation for Animals
Consensus Report

registered name of dog   registration no. (AKC, CKC)

breed   sex

color   Date of Birth

tattoo   Age at evaluation in months

Application number   Date of Report

owner

veterinarian

CONSENSUS OF THE RADIOGRAPHIC EVALUATIONS OF PELVIC PHENOTYPE WITH RESPECT TO CANINE HIP DYSPLASIA. THESE CATEGORIES ARE NOT ELIGIBLE FOR AN OFA BREED REGISTRY NUMBER.

_____ **BORDERLINE HIP JOINT CONFORMATION**
marginal hip joint conformation of indeterminate status with respect to hip dysplasia at this time

_____ **MILD HIP DYSPLASIA**
radiographic evidence of minor dysplastic change of the hip joints

_____ **MODERATE HIP DYSPLASIA**
well defined radiographic evidence of dysplastic changes of the hip joints

_____ **SEVERE HIP DYSPLASIA**
radiographic evidence of marked dysplastic changes of the hip joints

RADIOGRAPHIC FINDINGS

HIP JOINTS - STANDARD VD VIEW

_____ subluxation

_____ remodeling of femoral head/neck

_____ osteoarthritis/degenerative joint disease

_____ shallow acetabula

_____ acetabular rim/edge change

_____ unilateral pathology

_____ other _____

_____
E. A. CORLEY, D.V.M.
PROJECT DIRECTOR

Dysplasia Control Registry

FLEXED LATERAL VIEW

Anconeal Process

Coronoid Process

Humerus

Ulna

Radius

Sample OFA Consensus Report (Hips). Reprinted with permission.

Normal anatomy of the canine elbow joint. This is a flexed, lateral view.

13

FEMUR   **PELVIS**

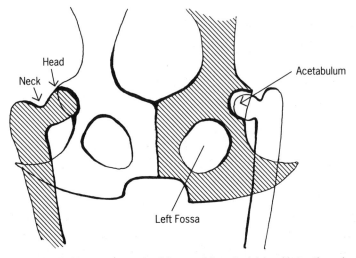

A normal hip (left) contrasted with a subluxated hip. Note the shallow acetabulum in the subluxated hip.

FEMORAL HEAD   **ACETABULUM**

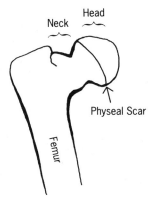
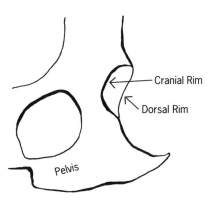

Configuration of the normal femoral head (left) and hip socket into which this bone fits.

of the hock and elbow may be needed to see an OCD lesion in these joints.

Although spontaneous recovery may occur, most individuals are best treated with surgery to remove diseased portions of the joint surface. Arthritis may develop within the joint if surgery is delayed. Again, OFA radiologists will evaluate radiographs of the shoulder, knee or hock for evidence of OCD.

Craniomandibular Osteopathy

Craniomandibular osteopathy (CMO) is a condition that causes abnormal and excessive growth of the joint of the lower jaw. It is seen most commonly in terriers between three and six months of age, although many other breeds have been afflicted with CMO. It commonly affects both sides of the jaw simultaneously. Puppies with CMO may have obvious swelling of the jaw, difficulty in opening the mouth and intermittent bouts of fever. Radiographs will confirm the diagnosis. Some dogs are so severely affected that euthanasia is the only humane treatment, while other dogs will have all evidence of the disease completely regress.

Hypertrophic Osteodystrophy

Hypertrophic osteodystrophy (HOD) is another disease that causes obvious bony enlargement and pain. It affects the long bones, and swelling is most commonly noted just above the pastern and hock joints. HOD affects rapidly growing, large-breed dogs, usually between three and seven months of age. Affected puppies may have intermittent bouts of fever. Many affected puppies are in so much pain that they are reluctant to stand or move. Nutrition and genetics are believed to interact in causing this disease. Affected dogs should be given pain relief and fed high-quality dog food. To date, treatment with vitamin C is of questionable value. Although some dogs recover spontaneously, other dogs develop permanent deformities.

Eosinophilic Panosteitis

Eosinophilic panosteitis, commonly referred to as panno by breeders, causes a shifting leg lameness in dogs between six and twenty-four months of age. Although German Shepherds are most commonly affected, many large-breed puppies develop panosteitis.

NORMAL HIP   **SUBLUXATED HIP**

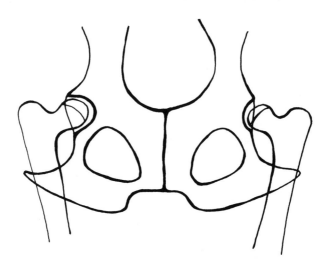

A normal hip is contrasted with a subluxated hip. Note the
shallow acetabulum in the subluxated hip.

NORMAL HIP   **DYSPLASTIC HIP**

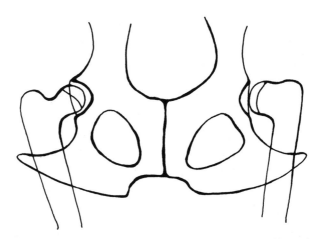

A normal hip is contrasted with a dysplastic hip. Note the
flattened femoral head and neck and the arthritic changes
in the dysplastic hip.

A radiograph will usually confirm the diagnosis of panosteitis. The central cavity of affected bones appears to be very dense on such radiographs. Analgesics are used to treat the associated pain. The disease will eventually resolve spontaneously.

Wobbler Syndrome

Wobbler syndrome is a disease caused by a malformation of the spinal bones in the neck region of certain large breeds of dogs. It most commonly affects young Great Danes and middle-aged Doberman Pinschers. Rear-leg clumsiness is most frequently noted. Plain radiographs sometimes will not reveal the malformation. In such cases, a myelogram is needed to diagnose and surgically treat the disease. When a myelogram is performed, dye is injected into the fluid surrounding the spinal cord to better outline the cord. Medical treatment with cage rest and steroids will help some patients. Other patients can be helped only with surgery, and not all surgical patients will recover adequately.

Atlantoaxial Subluxation

Atlantoaxial subluxation is a disease caused by a malformation of the spinal bones in the upper neck region of miniature breeds of dogs. All four limbs are affected and are weak and clumsy. Surgery to stabilize the neck bones is the only treatment.

Legg-Calve-Perthes' Disease

Legg-Calve-Perthes' disease is otherwise known as avascular necrosis of the femoral head. This disease causes destruction of the femoral head in small breeds of dogs. Usually only one leg is affected. Treatment is surgical removal of the affected femoral head.

Medial Patellar Luxation

Medial patellar luxation is a disease of the knee joint of small breeds of dogs. It is caused by a malformation of the hind limb. Most affected dogs are bowlegged. As a result, the kneecap does not sit on the central groove of the thighbone. Rather, it slips inwardly toward the center of the dog's body. The disease may affect

Orthopedic Foundation for Animals
Consensus Report
Elbows

registered name of dog

breed

color

tattoo

Application number

registration no. (AKC, CKC)

sex

Date of Birth

Age at evaluation in months

Date of Report

owner

veterinarian

RADIOGRAPHIC EVALUATION OF ELBOW PHENOTYPE WITH RESPECT TO ELBOW DYSPLASIA

ELBOW DYSPLASIA

Grade I   L_____ R_____
Grade II   L_____ R_____
Grade III   L_____ R_____

RADIOGRAPHIC FINDINGS

Degenerative Joint Disease (DJD)   L_____ R_____
Ununited Anconeal Process (UAP)   L_____ R_____
Fragmented Coronoid Process (FCP)   L_____ R_____
Osteochondrosis (OCD)   L_____ R_____

MISCELLANEOUS FINDINGS

_____ Previous Fracture

_____ _____

E. A. Corley, DVM
Project Director

Sample OFA Consensus Report (Elbows). Reprinted with permission.

18

one or both legs and may be seen in varying degrees of severity. Mildly affected dogs may live comfortably with the disease. They are usually seen to hop as they run along. This extra hopping step helps them to compensate for the displaced kneecap. Severely affected dogs require surgery to tighten the ligaments in the knee joint.

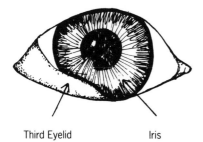

Third Eyelid   Iris

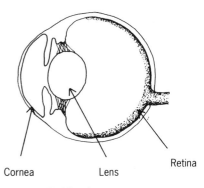

Cornea   Lens

Retina

Normal anatomy of the canine eye—front and side views.

2

The Canine Eye Registration Foundation

THE CANINE EYE REGISTRATION Foundation, Inc. (CERF) is a registry that records those dogs that physically appear to be free of heritable eye diseases. CERF differs from OFA in several respects. For one, dogs are not permanently registered with CERF. For another, different breeds have different age requirements regarding initial and subsequent evaluations. Like the OFA, CERF may classify a dog as "suspicious" and require reexamination in six months. And like OFA numbers, CERF numbers are coded to give information at a glance.

There are four parts to the code. The initial letters indicate breed. The following series of digits tells how many dogs of that breed have been evaluated. The next two digits indicate the year of the registration and the final two digits indicate the age of the dog in months at the time of the evaluation. For example, if you were to receive a CERF number of PO-100/82-18, you would have the one-hundredth Poodle to be registered. Your dog would have been registered in 1982 at an age of eighteen months.

Just as board-certified veterinary radiologists are required to interpret OFA films, board-certified veterinary ophthalmologists are required to examine eyes for CERF. Many people become familiar with CERF through "eye clinics" held by local breed clubs, at which an ophthalmologist will examine large numbers of dogs for a minimal fee. If you want to have your dog examined and cannot find an eye clinic in your area, contact your local veterinarian. He or she can direct you to the nearest veterinary ophthalmologist.

When veterinary ophthalmologists examine dogs for CERF, they thoroughly examine various parts of the eye, looking for a myriad of eye diseases that have a known or suspected heritable cause. This chapter will discuss heritable eye diseases by classifying them anatomically. Diseases of the normal eyelids, the third eyelid, the cornea, the retina and the lens will be discussed. Glaucoma will also be mentioned.

DISEASES OF THE EYELIDS

The most common heritable eye diseases are those that affect the eyelids. These include entropion, ectropion and distichiasis.

Entropion is seen in many breeds, but the Shar-Pei is probably the one breed most infamous for having problems with entropion. In essence, entropion results when the eyelid is drawn too tight, causing an inversion of the eyelid margin. The inverted margin in turn causes a constant irritation to the surface of the eye. Affected dogs tear excessively, and the condition is usually painful.

Ectropion is another disease of the eyelid. It is commonly seen in Clumber Spaniels, Saint Bernards and other breeds with loose facial skin. The eyelid droops excessively and forms a pocket for foreign material to accumulate into.

Distichiasis is a long name for abnormal eyelashes. The eyelashes grow inward toward the surface of the eye and cause constant irritation.

The cure for all these diseases is surgery. Prevention involves selective breeding to avoid these traits. Breeders should choose for breeding only dogs that have good eye conformation.

DISEASES OF THE THIRD EYELID

There are two known diseases of the third eyelid, and they are difficult for the inexperienced to distinguish. Cherry eye is very common, especially in American Cocker Spaniels. It occurs because

An American Cocker Spaniel with unilateral cherry eye.

A Chow Chow following surgery to correct entropion of the lower left eyelid. Note that this dog now has mild ectropion of the same eyelid.

A Chinese Shar-pei with entropion of the upper eyelids and ectropion of the lower eyelids.

Hair on the facial folds of short-faced breeds, such as this Pug, my come in direct contact with the surface of the eye, ultimately resulting in corneal ulcers.

the gland of the third eyelid enlarges dramatically. Scroll eye occurs when the cartilage located within the third eyelid curls. It is relatively uncommon. Again, the cure for these diseases is surgery, and prevention involves selective breeding.

DISEASES OF THE CORNEA

The surface of the eye is called the cornea and should be transparent. A few heritable diseases cause the cornea to become opaque. Pannus is a poorly understood disease occasionally seen in German Shepherd Dogs that causes a cloudy cornea. Exposure to sunlight worsens pannus; application of topical steroids alleviates pannus. Inheritance patterns are not known.

A laceration of the cornea is called a corneal ulcer. Boxers are prediposed to developing ulcers. The cause is unknown. Boxer ulcers tend to be recurrent. Untreated hypothyroid dogs are also likely to develop recurrent ulcers.

DISEASES OF THE RETINA

Most people use CERF to certify their breeding stock as free from retinal diseases. The retina is the back surface of the eye and is the part of the eye that actually receives visual input. Diseases of the retina thus cause visual disturbances. Two heritable diseases of the retina are recognized: progressive retinal atrophy (PRA) and Collie eye anomaly (CEA).

PRA is the best-known retinal disease, and there are actually two forms of it. One is central PRA. Dogs afflicted with central PRA have difficulty seeing stationary objects and see best in dim light. Most affected dogs begin showing signs of the disease between three and five years of age. The mode of inheritance of central PRA is not known. General PRA is the second form of PRA. Dogs afflicted with general PRA are characterized by night blindness, which eventually progresses to total blindness. They lose peripheral vision. The age of onset varies with breed, but in general occurs sooner than in central PRA.

General PRA is inherited as a simple autosomal recessive. Because it is a simple autosomal recessive trait, three groups of dogs exist. Dogs are either healthy (RR), healthy carriers (Rr) or affected

Progressive retinal atrophy in blind English Springer Spaniel.

Collie eye anomaly (CEA) is inherited as an autosomal recessive as with general PRA and is found in Collies and Shetland Sheepdogs.

ENTROPION

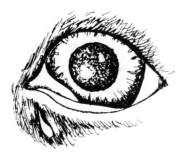
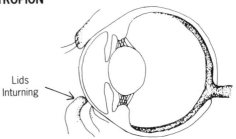

Lids
Inturning

ECTROPION

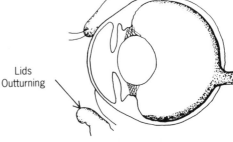

Lids
Outturning

DISTICHIASIS

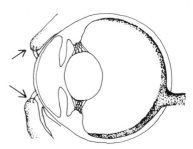

Hairs
Inturning

HERITABLE DISEASES OF THE EYELIDS: The eyelids of dogs affected with entropion (top) will turn inward. The eyelids of dogs affected with ectropion (center) will turn outward. Dogs affected with distichiasis (bottom) have inward-turning eyelashes causing constant irritation on the surface of the eye.

(rr). Eliminating a recessive gene from the population is very difficult because healthy carriers (Rr) can be detected only by test breedings. Several Irish Setter stud dogs have been proven to be healthy (RR) by test breedings done to affected (rr) bitches. Basic genetics shows that healthy males (RR) bred to affected (rr) bitches should produce all healthy carriers (Rr):

$$RR \times rr = Rr + Rr + Rr + Rr$$

Healthy carrier males (Rr) bred to affected (rr) bitches should produce 50 percent healthy carriers (Rr) and 50 percent affected (rr):

$$Rr \times rr = Rr + Rr + rr + rr$$

Anyone who has undertaken test breeding, also known as progeny testing, can attest that it is a long and arduous task. Blind bitches must be kept solely for the purpose of test breeding. Anything they produce will either be affected or carrying PRA and so must be removed from the breeding pool. And one test breeding does not produce enough puppies to statistically prove that the sire is indeed a healthy male (RR). Obviously, identifying carrier females is near impossible. Those who have undertaken progeny testing are to be commended for their efforts.

Collie eye anomaly is another well-known heritable disease of the retina. It affects Collies and Shetland Sheepdogs. In Collies it has been proven to be inherited as an autosomal recessive trait, just as in general PRA. As in hip dysplasia, a continuum of clinical signs exists and many people have tried to grade affected individuals. Grading dogs with CEA has little use except to note that those with a grade of 3, 4 or 5 are essentially blind. It is important to note that no affected dog (including those visual dogs given a grade of 1 or 2) should be bred because all grades carry the recessive gene. Unlike PRA and hip dysplasia, CEA is not progressive—that is, the signs associated with CEA do not worsen with time. Hence affected individuals can be detected at an early age. Affected puppies may be detected as early as six weeks of age, although a recheck examination in several months is recommended for further assurance.

'R Gang's Tiff of Button Ball, CD, owned by the author and bred by John Kane and John Childs, was examined by CERF in 1985. The certificate is shown below.

canine eye registration foundation, inc.

Rubin
EXAMINER

BREED	English Setter		CERF #	ES-217/85-68		
AKC REG. NAME	'R Gang's Tiff OF Button Ball		BIRTH DATE	Dec. 21, 1980		
AKC REG. NUMBER	SD56201	COLOR	orange belton		SEX	F
FILE NO.	B 37402	DATE EXAMINED	April 29, 1985	TATTOO IF ANY	None	
OWNERS NAME AND ADDRESS	Annette Carricato					
114 Greenwood Dr,		Middletown, PA,		17057		

®s

DISEASES OF THE LENS

The normal lens of the eye is transparent. A cloudy lens is abnormal and is called a cataract. Because a cataract is no longer transparent, vision in an eye affected with a cataract is impaired. Both congenital and juvenile cataracts are recognized in dogs.

Congenital cataracts are usually obvious by three months of age. As with many congenital diseases, they may or may not be inherited. Most are probably due to diseases during pregnancy.

Juvenile cataracts, on the other hand, are usually inherited. They appear before six years of age and progressively worsen. Miniature and Toy Poodles are most frequently affected. Other breeds that may be affected include the Afghan Hound, Labrador Retriever, Golden Retriever, Beagle, American Cocker Spaniel and Old English Sheepdog. Inheritance patterns may differ from one breed to the next.

Cataracts can be surgically removed to improve vision, unless another ocular disease exists simultaneously. Such is the case with many Poodles who suffer from both juvenile cataracts and PRA.

GLAUCOMA

Glaucoma is defined as an increased pressure within the eye. It is caused by an increased volume of fluid, which, in turn, is caused by a decreased flow of fluid out of the eye. Many breeds may be affected, most notably the American Cocker Spaniel and the Poodle. A persistent red-eyed appearance may be the first sign of glaucoma. Most affected dogs will have a large pupil, which will be painful. Pain is evidenced by excessive squinting and tearing. Glaucoma is definitively diagnosed by using an instrument known as a tonometer, which records the pressure within the eye. Various medications may be applied to the eye or given orally to treat glaucoma. Treatment is lifelong.

For further information on heritable eye diseases, you can write to: CERF, Purdue University, South Campus Court, Building C, West Lafayette, Indiana 47907. You can become a contributing member of CERF and receive newsletters and reports.

The normal heart pumps oxygenated blood throughout the body.

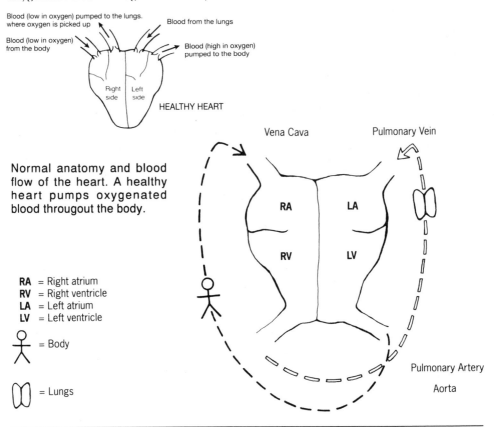

Blood (low in oxygen) pumped to the lungs. where oxygen is picked up

Blood from the lungs

Blood (low in oxygen) from the body

Blood (high in oxygen) pumped to the body

Right side | Left side

HEALTHY HEART

Normal anatomy and blood flow of the heart. A healthy heart pumps oxygenated blood througout the body.

Vena Cava

Pulmonary Vein

RA   LA

RV   LV

Pulmonary Artery

Aorta

RA = Right atrium
RV = Right ventricle
LA = Left atrium
LV = Left ventricle

= Body

= Lungs

common pathway

extrinsic system

intrinsic system

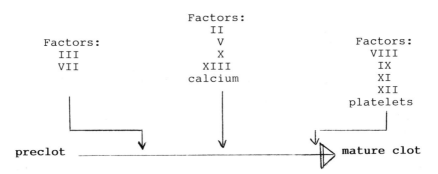

Factors:
II
V
X
XIII
calcium

Factors:
III
VII

Factors:
VIII
IX
XI
XII
platelets

preclot

mature clot

Normal clotting cascade. Many factors act in concert to cause clot formation. After W.J. Dodds and J.J. Kaneko, "Hemostatis and Blood Coagulation." In J.J. Kaneko and C.E. Cornelius, eds., *Clinical Biochemistry of Domestic Animals,* 2nd ed. Vol. II (New York: Academic Press, 1971).

3

Congenital Cardiovascular Diseases

NUMEROUS congenital cardiovascular diseases affect purebred dogs. Some affect the heart and its blood vessels, others affect the clotting system. Many of the diseases that disturb the heart are easily detected by auscultation—that is, they produce heart murmurs that can readily be heard with a stethoscope. However, some defects of the heart can be accurately detected only with the use of advanced diagnostics, such as electrocardiograms and ultrasound. Most of the diseases that disturb the clotting system require specialized blood testing in order to be detected.

INHERITED HEART DISEASES

A basic knowledge of the heart's anatomy and physiology is needed to understand common congenital heart diseases.

The heart can be divided into four chambers: right atrium, left atrium, right ventricle and left ventricle. The upper two chambers are the left and right atria. When blood flows back to the heart, it enters one of the atria. Blood is carried back to the atria in blood vessels called veins. The lower two chambers are the left and right ventricles. When blood leaves the heart, it exits from one of the two ventricles. Blood is carried away from the ventricles in blood vessels called arteries.

The left atrium is connected to the left ventricle by a valve called the mitral valve. The right atrium is connected to the right ventricle by a valve called the tricuspid valve. Normally, the atria are separated from one another, as are the ventricles.

The entire flow of blood to and from the heart is a continuous process. To understand the flow, it is convenient to start with blood that comes from the lungs. Blood coming back to the heart from the lungs is rich with oxygen. It enters the heart through a vessel known as the pulmonary vein. When oxygenated blood is returned to the heart, it enters the left atrium and is then pushed into the left ventricle. Blood leaves the left ventricle through a blood vessel called the aorta. The aorta is the artery that then supplies the body with a source of oxygen.

Ultimately, blood must be returned from the body to the lungs to restore its supply of oxygen. The vena cava is the blood vessel or vein that carries blood depleted of oxygen from the body back to the heart. Unoxygenated blood enters the right atrium. The heart pushes this blood from the right atrium into the right ventricle. From the right ventricle, unoxygenated blood leaves the heart from the pulmonary artery to travel to the lungs. In the lungs the blood regains its supply of oxygen. Thus the cycle is completed.

Most inherited heart diseases are due to defects in the anatomy of the heart. These anatomical defects ultimately cause functional defects.

If blood is caused to swirl with turbulence because of such a defect, a murmur will be heard. Murmurs are graded from I to VI, depending on how easily they can be heard. The loudness of a murmur cannot, however, be correlated to the severity of an underlying heart disease. Some murmurs are very distinctive in sound.

Murmurs can be defined according to when they are heard. Systolic murmurs are heard as the heart contracts. Diastolic murmurs are heard as the heart relaxes. Continuous murmurs are heard throughout the cycle of contraction and relaxation.

Murmurs can be further defined according to where they are heard the best. Usually, they are heard to be the loudest on either the right or the left side of a dog's chest.

Because murmurs may be caused by a variety of differing un-

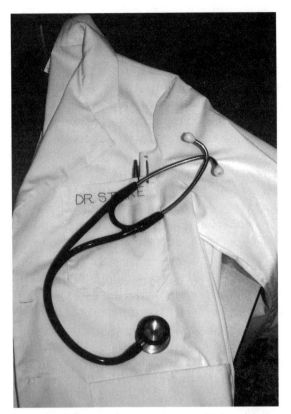

The familiar stethoscope is the simple tool the veterinarian uses to detect the presence of the heart murmur.

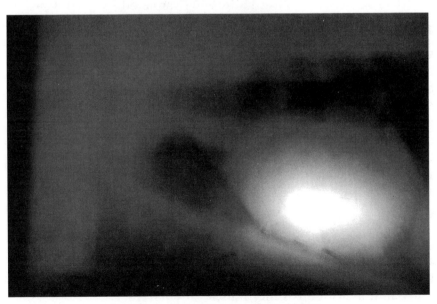

A radiograph showing an enlarged heart.

derlying diseases, further diagnostics are often needed to identify the particular underlying heart disease.

It is important to note that not every murmur heard in a puppy signifies disease. Some are innocent murmurs that dissipate as the puppy grows. A puppy that has a murmur should be auscultated periodically or should undergo a complete cardiac examination to identify any congenital heart disease. Physical examination of affected puppies may or may not reveal abnormalities other than a murmur. Affected puppies may have stunted growth, pale membranes, blue membranes, weak pulses, bounding pulses or jugular vein distention. Further diagnostic tests are indicated if the nature of a congenital heart defect underlying a murmur is to be found. Tests that may prove useful include radiographs, electrocardiograms and ultrasound.

Radiographs are most useful in identifying enlargement of the heart. Usually, enlargement can be defined as either right or left heart enlargement. Radiographs can also show other signs of heart disease, such as alterations in blood vessels.

An electrocardiogram (EKG) is taken to record electrical impulses generated by the heart. An EKG can be very useful in detecting an abnormal rhythm that may result from some heart diseases.

Ultrasound is used to produce an image of the heart and thereby detect many heart defects. Ultrasound may also be used to detect changes in blood flow that result from some heart defects.

The most common congenital heart defects recognized in dogs usually produce murmurs. They can often be further defined with radiographs and ultrasound. The most common defects include subaortic stenosis (SAS), pulmonic stenosis (PS), ventricular septal defect (VSD), patent ductus arteriosis (PDA), tetralogy of Fallot and persistent right aortic arch (PRAA). All except PRAA produce murmurs. Dilated cardiomyopathy does not produce a murmur and is not a congenital heart disease, but it is believed to be hereditary. Each of these conditions will be discussed in the following sections.

Subaortic Stenosis

Subaortic stenosis is due to a constriction of the aorta. This constriction makes it difficult for the heart to pump blood out of the left ventricle. As a result, the left heart must work harder than usual and, as with any other muscle, it enlarges.

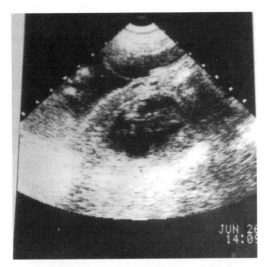

Ultrasound can produce images of the heart
to detect anatomical defects.

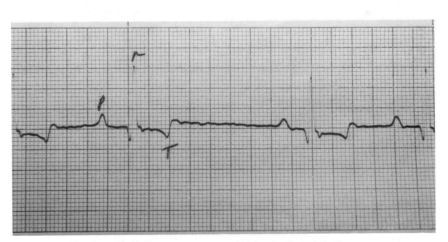

Electrocardiograms may reveal irregular heart rhythms.

The Newfoundland Spillways Katie Sue Nanjo, owned by John Stuckey and Nancy Bartlett, was determined to be free of subaortic stenosis by the use of ultrasound. *John Ashbey*

The constriction will cause turbulence, which will in turn produce a murmur. The murmur will be best heard on the left side of the chest because this is where the aorta lies. The murmur produced is a systolic murmur. Radiographs of affected dogs may reveal an enlarged left side of the heart. An EKG may reveal an enlarged left heart or an arrhythmia. Ultrasound can definitively diagnose most cases of SAS. The constriction itself may be noted or the abnormal flow may be detected.

SAS is seen most frequently in Boxers, German Shepherd Dogs, German Shorthaired Pointers and Newfoundlands. Affected dogs may show no signs, may faint or may die suddenly at a young age. Dogs with advanced cases may be prone to coughing, difficult breathing or fluid retention. Most affected puppies can be detected with auscultation. If any doubt exists, ultrasound should be pursued. Although surgical treatment is available, the prognosis is poor once signs are evident.

Pulmonic Stenosis

Pulmonic stenosis is caused by a narrowing of the pulmonary artery. This in turn constricts the outflow tract of the right ventricle, and as a result the right ventricle enlarges.

Like SAS, pulmonic stenosis causes a left-sided, systolic murmur. Radiographs and an EKG, however, will reveal right-sided enlargement if any signs are evident. Ultrasound may help to confirm the diagnosis.

Pulmonic stenosis is seen most frequently in Beagles, but has been found in Bulldogs, Fox Terriers, Chihuahuas, Samoyeds and Miniature Schnauzers.

Most puppies are asymptomatic and affected dogs may live to middle age with no adverse effects. If a puppy develops heart failure secondary to PS, it may show stunted growth, difficult breathing and exercise intolerance.

Surgery is available to treat most cases of pulmonic stenosis, although the prognosis is poor.

Ventricular Septal Defect

VSD is caused by a hole in the wall that normally divides one ventricle from another. As a result, blood passes from the left ventricle to the right ventricle. Normally blood would pass from the

Pulmonic stenosis appears in a variety of unrelated breeds but is most frequently noted in the Beagle.

Ventricular septal defect, as described in the text, eventually results in the enlargement of the ventricle. The condition has been noted in Bulldogs.

The Pomeranian is one of the breeds known to be predisposed to patent ductus arteriosis (PDA).

left ventricle out through the aorta. Subsequently the right ventricle enlarges.

No signs are seen with small defects. Larger defects produce a systolic murmur best heard on the right side of the chest. Radiographs and EKGs may reveal right heart enlargement. Corrective surgery may be performed if the defect is large.

Ventricular septal defect is found in the Bulldog.

Patent Ductus Arteriosis

PDA is the most common congenital heart defect recognized to occur in dogs. It is the result of abnormal neonatal development of the heart. Blood continues to flow in affected puppies as it did before birth. Since a fetus receives oxygen from its mother, it does not need to send blood to its lungs. A neonate, however, must shift the pattern of blood flow so that the lungs can receive oxygen. Normally, the ductus arteriosis is closed shortly after birth. In dogs with PDA, the ductus arteriosis remains patent.

Individual dogs may be affected in a variety of ways. Some puppies will fade. Other puppies will live six or eight weeks only to die suddenly. Most puppies who survive to eight weeks will survive to adulthood. They may or may not be subject to recurrent bouts of heart failure.

PDA produces a distinctive murmur described as a machinery murmur. The murmur is continuous and is best heard on the left side of the dog. Diagnostic tests may show an enlarged heart.

Breeds known to be predisposed to PDA include the Poodle, German Shepherd, Collie, Shetland Sheepdog and Pomeranian.

Tetralogy of Fallot

Tetralogy of Fallot is actually a combination of three separate defects. The three defects that combine to produce tetralogy are PS, VSD and an abnormally positioned aorta.

Tetralogy of Fallot is usually recognized in young dogs. Affected puppies may collapse after exercise. They have blue gums because their blood is not well oxygenated. A left-sided, systolic murmur is heard. Diagnostic tests may reveal an enlarged right heart.

This disease is recognized in the Keeshond and Bulldog.

Open heart surgery is available to treat some cases.

The Keeshond is one of the breeds in which tetralogy of Fallot has been recognized.

The German Shepherd Dog is one of the breeds most often affected by persistent right aortic arch (PRAA).

Persistent Right Aortic Arch

PRAA is due to a developmental defect in the aorta. A remnant of the fetal aorta remains in affected puppies. This remnant wraps around the esophagus, which delivers food from the mouth to the stomach.

No murmur is heard as a result of PRAA. Signs of PRAA are referable to the damage done to the esophagus. Affected dogs often cannot properly transport food to the stomach. As a result, food is often regurgitated. Radiographs are used to identify the abnormal esophagus.

Dogs with PRAA may be treated surgically. The constricting band of residual aorta must be transected. Dogs must often be fed at an elevated height even after surgery to help ease the passage of food.

PRAA most often affects German Shepherds and Irish Setters.

Dilated Cardiomyopathy

Dilated cardiomyopathy is caused by disease of the muscle of the heart and is suspected to have a hereditary basis.

Radiographs of affected dogs show an enlarged heart, and EKGs usually show abnormalities. Ultrasound will reveal the diseased state of the muscle wall.

Dilated cardiomyopathy is seen in large breeds of dogs between three and eight years of age. Males are affected more often than are females. Affected dogs are debilitated and have a distended abdomen.

The prognosis for any dog diagnosed with dilated cardiomyopathy is very grave. Most dogs die within six to twelve months after diagnosis. Nonspecific medical treatment may be used to treat congestive heart failure.

INHERITED BLEEDING DISORDERS

Hereditary bleeding disorders are caused by a clotting factor deficiency, a platelet malfunction or a combination of both. The process of blood clotting is a cascading event with many intermediate steps. Each step is regulated by a separate compound, referred to as a factor. A deficiency in any one of these factors will interrupt the cascading sequence and prohibit normal blood clotting. Many different factors are known to be required for the sequence to occur. Each factor is numbered and given an individual name. Diseases causing clotting abnormalities likewise are named according to the factor that is deficient. Three bleeding disorders that are due to factor deficiencies are commonly recognized in dogs: hemophilia A, hemophilia B and von Willebrand's disease.

Hemophilia A, referred to as classic hemophilia, is caused by a factor VIII deficiency. It is probably the most common disorder and is recognized in practically all breeds of dogs and in mongrels.

Hemophilia B is caused by a factor IX deficiency and is also referred to as Christmas hemophilia. It has been reported in Cairn Terriers, Coonhounds, Saint Bernards, Cocker Spaniels, French Bulldogs and Alaskan Malamutes.

Hemophilia A and B are both inherited as sex-linked traits. This means that they are usually only manifested in the male. Affected males are produced when carrier bitches are bred to normal stud dogs. Both affected male and female puppies will result when carrier bitches are bred to affected stud dogs.

The normal clotting sequence is also dependent upon a type of blood cell called the platelet or thrombocyte. If platelets do not function properly, the blood will not clot properly. Hereditary thrombocytopathia is the term given to inherited bleeding disorders due to abnormal platelet function. Thrombocytopathia is recognized in two forms in each of two breeds, the Otterhound and the Basset Hound. Other breeds may be affected.

Von Willebrand's disease is caused by both a factor deficiency and a platelet dysfunction. It is not a sex-linked trait. It is, however, very common and is known to affect many breeds. The breeds most commonly affected include the Golden Retriever, Miniature Schnauzer, German Shepherd Dog, Doberman Pinscher and Scottish Terrier.

Signs of the disease vary with the particular disorder and the individual affected. Carrier dogs are more mildly affected. Some dogs only exhibit signs after trauma or surgery. Other dogs may exhibit spontaneous bleeding episodes evidenced by bloody urine, bloody feces or swollen joints. Bleeding into joint cavities is noted frequently in hemophiliacs. A crisis may be precipitated by administering aspirin or modified-live vaccines.

Definitive diagnosis requires specialized blood testing. Some disorders can only be diagnosed by laboratories specializing in re-

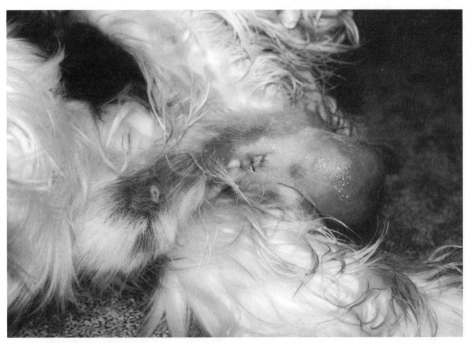

Von Willebrand's disease is a bleeding disorder that has been noted in a wide variety of breeds. Dogs suffering with VWD will bleed excessively after routine surgery. Shown here is a scrotal hematoma that developed following castration of an English Springer Spaniel.

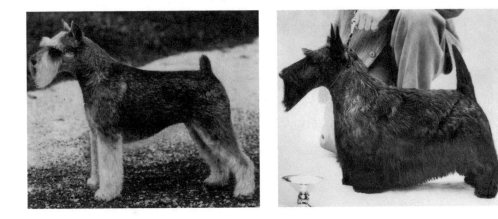

Owner of dogs from breeds commonly affected by von Willebrand's disease, such as the Miniature Schnauzer, Scottish Terrier and Golden Retriever, must be constantly vigilant to the various symptoms that may appear.

search on clotting diseases. It is important to note that both normal and carrier states can be identified. Both affected and carrier animals should be identified and removed from the breeding pool. Consult your veterinarian to discuss which laboratory screening tests are currently available.

There is no cure for any of the bleeding disorders. Affected dogs may be treated with fresh blood transfusions when emergencies arise, and care must always be taken to minimize stress. Animals with mild defects may lead a relatively normal life. However, lifelong treatment of hemophilia is difficult in severe cases.

The symptoms of cerebellar abiotrophy are manifested at different ages among the known affected breeds. In Kerry Blue Terriers symptoms will appear when puppies are between eight and sixteen weeks old.   *Rudolph Tauskey*

The onset of clinical signs of cerebellar abiotrophy in Gordon Setters does not occur until the affected dog is between six and thirty months old.

4

Inherited Neurological Diseases

NEUROLOGICAL DISEASES are those that affect the brain, the spinal cord or the peripheral nerves. A multitude of neurological diseases are known or suspected to be inherited in dogs. Fortunately, few are commonly seen. Inherited neurological diseases that occur commonly in dogs are cerebellar abiotrophy, deafness, epilepsy, hydrocephalus and intervertebral disk disease. Cerebellar abiotrophy, epilepsy and hydrocephalus affect the brain. Intervertebral disk disease affects the spinal cord. Hereditary deafness in dogs is believed to be due to disease of the peripheral nerve that senses sound. Each of these diseases will be discussed in the following sections.

CEREBELLAR ABIOTROPHY

The cerebellum is the part of the brain that controls the co-ordination of bodily movements. Cerebellar abiotrophy is an inherited disease that causes the cerebellum to degenerate. The signs of cerebellar abiotrophy include a rigid, goose-stepping gait, head tremors and a broad-based stance.

In general, this condition grows progressively worse. Many

different breeds may be affected. Each breed appears to have a different age for the onset of clinical signs. Rough Collies and Bullmastiff puppies usually display signs between four and eight weeks of age. Kerry Blue Terriers begin to show signs between eight and sixteen weeks of age. A late onset of clinical signs is noted in Gordon Setters. In this breed, the signs usually begin to appear between six and thirty months of age.

The diagnosis of cerebellar abiotrophy is based on clinical signs. There is no treatment and the prognosis is very poor.

DEAFNESS

Deafness is the inability to hear sound from one or both ears. It may be acquired or inherited. Severe head trauma, chronic ear infections or senility may cause acquired deafness. Genetic deafness may occur in any breed of dog. However, it is most commonly associated with white coat color and pigmentation disorders such as the merle gene. Breeds commonly affected include the Border Collie, Boston Terrier, Bull Terrier, Collie, Dalmatian, English Setter and Old English Sheepdog.

Most bilaterally deaf dogs display obvious signs of hearing deficiencies. Unilaterally deaf dogs do not. Because a dog may be deaf in one ear and hear normally from the other ear, an accurate diagnosis of deafness can be difficult to obtain. An electrophysiological method is available in limited locations to test for unilateral deafness. The test is commonly referred to as a BEAR test. BEAR stands for "brain stem evoked auditory response." To conduct the test, a probe is placed within the ear in question and sounds are transmitted. A receiver is used to detect whether or not the brain responds to the transmitted sounds. Puppies can be tested as young as six weeks of age. Deafness may be misdiagnosed if a severe ear infection is present. If such a misdiagnosis is suspected, the dog should be tested again after the ear infection is resolved.

Hearing deficits due to genetic deafness are usually present at birth and are permanent. There is no cure for congenital deafness and the prognosis is therefore poor.

Genetic deafness can occur in any breed, but it is most commonly associated with white dogs or dogs having pigmentation disorders. Among the breeds commonly diagnosed with deaf individuals are Boston Terriers (above) and white Bull Terriers (below).

EPILEPSY

Epilepsy is an idiopathic disease that causes seizures in dogs. Although idiopathic means that the cause is unknown, epilepsy is suspected to have a genetic cause.

A seizure is defined as a sudden period of abnormal, involuntary behavior. Usually, affected dogs are unconscious during the seizure and manifest uncontrolled muscle activity. When a grand mal seizure occurs, the entire body is involved. A dog in a grand mal seizure will lie flat on its side, paddle its legs and chew uncontrollably. Petit mal seizures are those that cause a loss of consciousness without involuntary muscle movements. These seizures may be difficult to distinguish from fainting episodes.

It is important to note that a seizure is a sign of disease and not a definitive diagnosis, since many diseases will cause dogs to have seizures. Idiopathic epilepsy is one such disease. Diseases other than epilepsy that may cause seizure activity include severe head trauma, lead poisoning and eclampsia. Most often, however, a specific cause for the seizure activity cannot be found.

If no infectious, metabolic or toxic problem can be found to explain repeated seizure episodes, idiopathic epilepsy is presumed. An electroencephalogram (EEG) can record electrical impulses across the brain and can sometimes be used to confirm a diagnosis of idiopathic epilepsy.

Treatment involves lifelong medical therapy with anticonvulsant drugs. Most dogs gradually adapt to the drugs and need larger and larger doses with time. The prognosis is poor, as the seizures may become uncontrolled even with progressively larger doses of anticonvulsant drugs.

HYDROCEPHALUS

Hydrocephalus is usually translated as "water on the brain." Actually, hydrocephalus is a condition in which too much fluid accumulates within the ventricles of the brain. The ventricles are pockets within the brain that make and store fluid used to surround and protect the brain.

Hydrocephalus is a congenital disease that can usually be diagnosed at birth simply by the appearance of affected puppies. Affected puppies will appear to have enlarged, dome-shaped heads. They may survive and exhibit neurological signs of disease as they

50

Any breed can be affected with hydrocephalus, or water on the brain. This is a congenital condition and breeders who work with breeds having dome-shaped heads should be careful to determine whether newborns have normal domes or if an individual is indeed hydrocephalic.

Spinal Bones

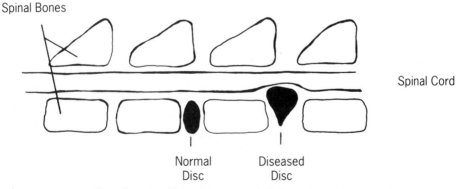

Spinal Cord

Normal
Disc

Diseased
Disc

INTERVERTEBRAL DISK DISEASE: When a ruptured disk impinges on the spinal cord, signs of intervertebral disk disease result.

Intervertebral disk disease has been seen in a number of breeds but is well-known in middle-aged individuals of long-backed breeds. Dachshunds (above) and Dandie Dinmont Terriers (below) are often affected. The therapy may be conservative or more involved, depending on the severity of the condition and the location of the ruptured disks.

age. Usually, they have an uncoordinated gait, are mentally dull and develop seizures. The diagnosis can be confirmed by injecting dye into the fluid and taking a radiograph of the skull.

There is no cure for hydrocephalus. Steroids seem to be somewhat helpful in diminishing fluid production in some dogs. As time progresses, anticonvulsant medication may be necessary for the treatment of many dogs. The prognosis is poor.

INTERVERTEBRAL DISK DISEASE

Intervertebral disk disease is a disease of the disks that lie between the bones of the spine. Affected disks migrate from their normal position between bones and impinge on the spinal cord. As a result of the impingement, varying symptoms may be evident.

The disease tends to occur in either the cervical or the thoracolumbar regions. When disks in the cervical or neck region are diseased, they cause pain. Affected dogs are reluctant to raise their heads and subsequently refrain from jumping onto furniture.

When disks in the thoracolumbar region are affected, they cause immobility. Varying degrees of rear limb paralysis may be seen. Some dogs lose all control of their rear limbs.

Intervertebral disk disease tends to recur. It may affect the cervical region in one episode and the thoracolumbar region in the next episode or vice versa. The disease is seen most frequently in middle-aged, long-backed breeds of dogs. Cage rest and steroids may treat some dogs effectively. Other dogs require corrective surgery in which the offending disk or disks are removed.

All dogs are exposed to mites in a normal environment. Disease will occur only when abnormal skin is involved. *Sanderson*

5

Heritable Skin Diseases

MANY BREEDS of dogs have a known or suspected heritable predisposition for certain skin diseases. Most of these diseases are an extreme nuisance to both the dog and the owner. Some of these diseases, however, can actually be fatal. Although we can often manage many of these problems, we would be best served by avoiding them in the first place by the use of selective breeding. This section discusses heritable skin diseases by classifying them as parasitic, hormonal, nutritional, allergic and autoimmune.

PARASITIC SKIN DISEASES

Demodectic mange is caused by a cigar-shaped, microscopic mite known as *Demodex canis*. The mite is a normal inhabitant of healthy canine skin. Disease occurs only when the dog's skin is abnormal, thus allowing the mite to proliferate. The mites live within hair follicles and cause hair loss. A veterinarian can perform a skin scraping to determine whether mites are present.

Two forms of the disease exist. Localized demodex is the most common form. It is seen in puppies and usually affects the head. In addition to the bald spot or spots on their heads, many of these puppies experience hair loss around the eyes, giving them the appearance of wearing spectacles. Affected puppies are not itchy; they simply lose hair. Most dogs that develop generalized demodex, the second form of the disease, did not start with localized demodex. Generalized demodex affects the dog's entire body in a diffuse manner. Often the skin is secondarily infected and the dog becomes very itchy. Sometimes people refer to this as red mange.

Puppies with localized demodex usually self-cure with time. Dogs with generalized demodex almost never return to normal, even after frequent and repeated treatments of medicated baths, dips and antibiotics. Bulldogs and the setter breeds have a known familial tendency to develop red mange.

HORMONAL SKIN DISEASES

A number of heritable hormonal skin diseases are recognized in dogs: hypothyroidism, Cushing's disease, pituitary dwarfism and sex hormone imbalances. Dogs affected with hormonal skin diseases go bald without scratching at themselves. Classically, the trunk of the body is affected while the head and legs remain normal. Although the genetics of most of these diseases are unknown, obvious breed tendencies are evident. Hypothyroidism and Cushing's disease are relatively common; pituitary dwarfism and sex hormone imbalances are relatively rare.

Hypothyroidism

Hypothyroidism is caused by the insufficient production of thyroid hormone, or thyroxine. It is relatively common. No one knows for certain what causes the thyroid gland to decrease its production of thyroxine, but a genetic component is strongly suspected because certain breeds are infamous for having problems associated with hypothyroidism. Doberman Pinschers, Golden Retrievers and Beagles are predisposed. It appears that the dog's immune system goes haywire and starts to produce antibodies against its own thyroid gland. Dr. Jean Dodds has reported an association between hypothyroidism and von Willebrand's disease.

Signs of hypothyroidism include lethargy, hair loss, intolerance of cold weather, irregular estrous cycles and prolonged anestrus. Any combination of signs may occur. Most dogs begin showing signs as young adults two to four years of age. Since the signs are so

Localized demodex in a Gordon Setter evidenced by hair loss around the eyes.

The same dog exhibiting spots of hair loss on top of the skull.

variable and sometimes very subtle, the disease can be accurately diagnosed only through blood testing.

Dogs are screened for hypothyroidism by measuring levels of thyroxine circulating in the bloodstream. The thyroid gland actually produces two hormones: triiodothyroxine (T3) and tetraiodothyroxine (T4). The only physical difference between the two hormones is that T3 has three iodine molecules attached to it while T4 has four. Most of the body's thyroid hormone is circulated in the bloodstream as T4. It is believed that T4 is converted to T3 before cells absorb and use the hormone.

Most thyroid hormone is carried around in the blood by a carrier protein. The portion of thyroxine that is carried by a protein is referred to as the bound fraction. The rest is referred to as unbound. Four different components can thus be measured: bound T4, unbound T4, bound T3 and unbound T3. Most laboratories can measure only total T4 and total T3. Most veterinarians feel that this is adequate. Some veterinarians, however, believe that certain lines of dogs have problems solely with deficiencies of unbound portions.

Most veterinarians measure resting total T4. If hypothyroidism is strongly suspected and the resting total T4 is normal, a TSH stimulation test can be performed. Please refer to Figure 5-1. This is a test in which T4 is measured both before and several hours after the dog is injected with TSH. TSH is a naturally occurring hormone that stimulates the normal thyroid gland to produce two to three times the amount of resting T4. Truly hypothyroid dogs respond abnormally to TSH.

normal value ○

normal range ○—TSH stimulation

bound T4   abnormal value △

abnormal range △

○ = dog with a normal thyroid gland

△ = dog with an abnormal thyroid gland

Figure 5-1 Evaluating Thyroid Function

One final blood test can be taken to evaluate hypothyroid dogs. This test measures the amount of antithyroid antibodies (ATA). Normal dogs will make very small quantities of antibodies against their own thyroid gland. However, most hypothyroid dogs produce a large quantity of ATA.

Hypothyroidism is treated with hormone replacement. Affected dogs must be given medication for the rest of their lives. Synthetic hormones seem to be superior to naturally occurring hormones because they are much more stable. Some hypothyroid dogs do not respond to therapy if generic drugs are used. Although some dogs respond to once-daily medication, most require twice-daily medication.

Cushing's Disease

Cushing's disease is a hormonal disease that causes skin manifestations. It is caused by an overabundance of adrenal steroid hormones. Sometimes it is naturally occurring; sometimes it occurs because the dog has been given long-term steroid therapy. Naturally occurring Cushing's disease shows breed predispositions. Poodles are most commonly diagnosed with Cushing's disease.

Signs of Cushing's include an insatiable thirst, increased urination, hair loss and a potbelly. These dogs are prone to developing all kinds of infections, especially of the skin and bladder.

Many tests have been designed to diagnose Cushing's disease in dogs. Currently, the most acceptable test is the low-dose dexamethasone suppression test. This test is similar to the TSH stimulation test in that hormone levels are measured both before and after an injection is given. With the low-dose dexamethasone suppression test, blood cortisol levels are measured both before and after an injection of dexamethasone. The level of cortisol should be lower after the injection. If not, the dog has Cushing's disease.

Unlike the thyroid gland, the adrenal gland produces many different types of steroid hormones. Thus, therapy can be both complicated and difficult.

Pituitary Dwarfism

Pituitary dwarfism is a rare disease that primarily affects German Shepherd Dogs. Affected dogs have deficiencies of all of the many pituitary hormones. As a result, they have stunted growth and abnormal haircoats. They retain their puppy coats throughout their shortened lifespans. Dogs afflicted with pituitary dwarfism show obvious symptoms, so no special diagnostics are required to detect the disease. Treatment involves complicated hormone replacement therapy and is often futile.

Sex Hormone Imbalances

The category of sex hormone imbalances actually encompasses several poorly understood syndromes. These include testosterone deficiency in male dogs, excessive estrogen in male dogs and ovarian imbalance in female dogs.

Testosterone deficiency can occur in both intact and castrated dogs. Replacement hormone therapy sometimes effectively treats these dogs. If the affected dog is intact, castration may help.

Excessive estrogen in male dogs is usually caused by testicular tumors and is most often seen in cryptorchid dogs. Affected dogs show classical signs. They have enlarged breasts and hair loss primarily around their necks. The skin darkens dramatically wherever hair is lost.

Ovarian imbalance plagues many bitches. Affected bitches notoriously blow their coats just after estrus. Several protocols for hormone replacement have been used to treat ovarian imbalance, but all have potentially serious side effects.

NUTRITIONAL SKIN DISEASES

Two types of nutritional deficiencies that cause skin disease are believed to have a heritable basis. They are zinc deficiency and vitamin A deficiency. Apparently, affected dogs cannot absorb adequate quantities of the nutrient even though their diet contains adequate amounts.

Heritable vitamin A deficiency is extremely rare and has been reported to primarily affect American Cocker Spaniels. These dogs have hair loss and dandruff on their faces.

Heritable zinc deficiency is also rare and has been reported to affect Alaskan Malamutes and Siberian Huskies. These dogs have severe crusting and are itchy. The face and the legs are affected on mature animals. Adult dogs with zinc deficiency may also have concurrent hypothyroidism. Young puppies usually have a more generalized distribution of lesions and also have lymph node enlargement.

Treatment involves giving large doses of the deficient nutrient.

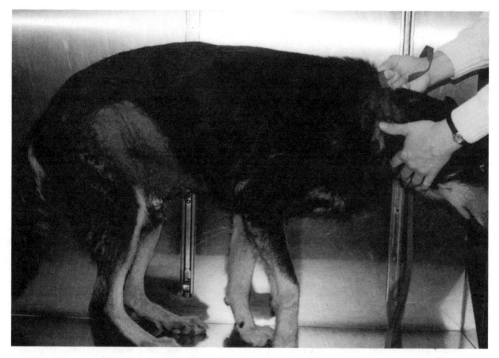

Estrogen deficiency in a German Shepherd Dog with hair loss on the flanks and neck. Note that the skin has darkened where the hair has fallen out. Following castration, this dog made a complete recovery.

ALLERGIC SKIN DISEASES

Three types of allergies commonly seen in dogs are flea, food and inhalant. Allergic dogs are itchy and, therefore, have many secondary skin and coat problems. They often have severe dandruff, which gives them an unpleasant odor. Hair loss results from constant biting and scratching. Steroids usually alleviate the itchiness dramatically.

Flea Allergy

Flea allergy is by far the most common type of allergy seen in dogs. Dogs infested with fleas behave classically. When they chew on themselves, they look as though they are nibbling corn on the cob. They bite and chew excessively at the back of their thighs, the base of their tails and the end of their backs. While fleas can make any dog miserable, fleas cause an excessive reaction in allergic dogs because the fleas' saliva causes a hypersensitivity reaction within the skin.

Food Allergy

Food allergies are rarely seen in dogs, possibly because the diagnosis is so difficult to prove. To prove that a dog is allergic to a certain food, it must be given a diet exclusively made of lamb and rice for at least two weeks. At the end of the two weeks, the dog should be free of itchiness; if allergic, the dog will become quite itchy once more when reintroduced to the original food. Most affected dogs do not respond well to steroids.

Inhalant Allergy

Dogs that are allergic to inhaled pollens are referred to as atopics. Dogs are quite different from people who are allergic to inhaled pollens. Dogs have mast cells in their skin rather than in their sinuses. Thus, when allergens are inhaled, these mast cells release histamines that make the dog very itchy. Unfortunately, most atopics respond very poorly to antihistamines. Steroids, on the other hand, usually make them quite comfortable. Complete allergy testing and desensitization programs are available for severe atopics. Atopics usually have a seasonal allergy that eventually progresses

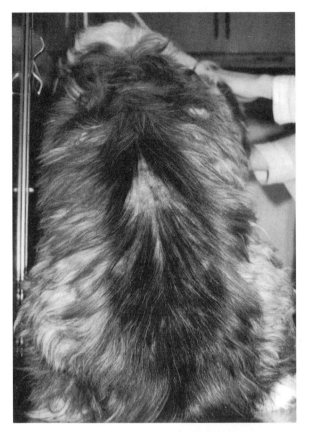

Dogs vary in allergic response to flea bites. Some hardly notice, while others will react strongly to just one bite. This Old English Sheepdog shows considerable hair loss as an obvious symptom.

Shetland Sheepdogs and Collies are subject to an autoimmune condition as described in the text.

to a year-round problem. Many breeds, including Dalmatians, Poodles and various terriers and setters, are predisposed to inhalant allergies.

AUTOIMMUNE SKIN DISEASES

A group of diseases referred to as pemphigus or pemphigus-like dermatoses have an autoimmune basis—that is, the dog's own body begins to destroy itself. Most of these diseases cause severe ulcerations, often around the mouth. Three of these diseases affect Collies and Shetland Sheepdogs: bullous pemphigoid, epidermolysis bullosa and systemic lupus. Mild cases can be managed with steroid therapy. Severe cases carry a poor prognosis. Fortunately, autoimmune skin diseases are rare.

6

Evaluation of Temperament

POOR TEMPERAMENT, whether in the English Setter or in any other breed, is one fault that I consider a major fault. Granted, good setter temperament is not good Sheltie temperament, and each breed has its own behavioral characteristics that lend type to the breed. However, breeders should remember two universal truths. One is that most puppies are sold to pet homes and should have temperaments suitable to being good pets. The second is that dogs with poor temperaments show poorly. Dogs that either lack self-confidence or have no inhibition about biting people simply cannot be shown.

Have you ever been foolish enough to try to show a potential fear-biter or a dominant aggressive dog? I was—once. I've seen dogs given second place in a class of one because they were timid. I've also seen dogs excused because they tried to bite the judge. Each of the handlers looked equally disappointed. There is certainly no need to go looking for disappointment in the breed ring.

Ask your veterinarian for an honest opinion of your dog. Veterinarians see hundreds of dogs at fifteen-minute intervals and either learn to size up temperament quickly or learn to take their licks. Your veterinarian can tell very quickly whether your dog is a po-

Owned by Bradford Wood, M.D., Ch. Sanroyale's Yves du Sabre, UDT, HIC, AD, TT, is a Belgian Tervuren that has made his presence felt in many phases of competition.

Ch. Marcy's Teddy Bear, CDX, HOF, owned by Marcy Zingler, is a multiple Group winner and the only individual admitted to the Keeshond Hall of Fame on conformation points that also holds an advanced obedience degree.

The two examples shown here are eloquent proof that dogs can be successfully shown in conformation and obedience—a credit to their breeds, their training and the people who believe in them.

tential fear-biter or a dominant aggressive. No need to waste entry fees.

Because you live with your dogs, you may be the best judge of their temperaments. You know which males fence-fight with other males. You know which bitches have to be held on a tight lead ringside. And you also know which dog adds the greatest joy to your daily life-style.

On the other hand, you may be the worst judge of their temperaments. My favorite male says hello by jumping on my shoulders and nibbling my ear. This tickles me pink and repulses all but my most dog-loving friends. I know of one breeder who houses his dogs in individual runs. His dogs are marvelous with people but vicious with other dogs. I could never own one of his dogs because all my dogs run together; however, most pet owners own only one dog and they adore his dogs. Try very hard to be objective when evaluating the temperament of your own dogs.

Some people use the Temperament Test to evaluate their dogs. Personally, I think that the test is relevant only to the Schutzhund breeds. So what if a Pomeranian is gun-shy? I'm inclined to believe that the test is gaining in popularity not because of its usefulness but, rather, because our quest for titles is gaining popularity. Please feel free to investigate the test and form your own opinion. For further information, please write to the American Temperament Testing Society, Inc., 13680 Van Nuys Boulevard, Pacoima, California 91331.

I find that simple obedience training teaches me a lot about my dogs. Consider trying it.

Everyone should read and reread their breed standard. Often it succinctly describes the ideal breed temperament. After reading the standard, make a list of temperament faults and memorize it. Then remember the adage "Like begets like."

Ch. BJ's Ultimate Sunrise, CD, owned by Brenda Parsons, D.V.M., and co-bred by her with Charlene Kickbush D.V.M., and handled here by Tom Greer, shows why champion show dogs are a hedge against many genetic disorders. *Alverson*

7

Championships

THE TITLE of AKC champion is an effective screen for many genetic disorders and often is undervalued. We all know that no dog can obtain its championship if it is cryptorchid or if it has an improper bite. However, we often forget that the title also acts as a screen for many maladies that we take for granted or overlook. For example, breed color is a genetic trait that is evaluated in the breed ring. No Gordon Setter can obtain its championship without possessing the Gordon's typical black-and-tan pattern of coloration. As a result, solid red Gordon Setters are not registered, shown or bred.

The title also screens for characteristics that are much more subtle. For example, English Setters are required to have eyes that are "bright, mild, intelligent and dark brown in color." Since English Setters with droopy lower eyelids have expressions that are anything but "intelligent," English Setters with ectropion do not fare well in the breed ring. And, as previously mentioned, the title effectively screens out dogs with gross temperament flaws.

PART TWO

Understanding Canine Reproduction

THE ULTIMATE GOAL of any breeding program is to produce sound puppies. Producing sound puppies can sometimes present a great number of challenges, however. By knowing something about canine reproduction, you can enhance your odds of success. This section was written to provide you with some basic information about canine reproduction. Hopefully, this information will help you avert many potential problems and solve the unavoidable ones.

8

Breeding Management

BREEDING MANAGEMENT can be optimized only with appropriate forethought and planning. By working with a licensed veterinarian, dog breeders can improve both the quantity and quality of the puppies they produce. Before breeding, each bitch should visit a veterinarian for a general physical examination and a brucellosis test. Likewise, stud dogs should ideally be examined and tested for brucellosis on a regular basis.

Breeders can also improve their success rate by learning all there is to know about the correct timing of breedings. Being able to both objectively and subjectively evaluate a bitch's estrous cycle will enable breeders to determine exactly when to breed a bitch.

Finally, by working with a veterinarian and learning what techniques are currently available, many breeders may benefit from the use of artificial insemination.

This chapter will discuss the many ways you can work with your veterinarian to properly plan breedings and maximize canine fertility.

PREBREEDING PHYSICAL EXAMINATION

A general physical examination performed one to three months prior to breeding will allow veterinarians and breeders to work together and plan breedings. Bitches should be examined approximately one month prior to breeding unless they cycle irregularly; such bitches should be examined one to three months before breeding.

A veterinarian can provide an objective opinion of the bitch's overall condition. Sometimes fanciers prefer to look at Afghan Hounds that are a little underweight and at Basset Hounds that are a little overweight. An objective professionial opinion will suggest whether a bitch should be fattened up or slimmed down. Sometimes it is difficult to evaluate coat condition. Saving a penny on dog food can cost a dollar in dog nutrition. An obvious parasite problem may not be so obvious.

A fecal sample should be tested on the day of the physical, as this is the appropriate time to treat a bitch for intestinal parasites. A bitch should never be given any unnecessary medications during pregnancy. Drugs should especially be avoided during the first trimester because this is when the embryos are most likely to be harmed. If necessary, a composite fecal sample can be taken from several dogs. Any sample that is tested should be freshly collected. If need be, a veterinarian can perform a rectal to collect a fresh sample.

If there is a problem with external parasites (that is, fleas), the same rules of thumb should be followed.

The ideal time to vaccinate a bitch is one month before breeding. She will have maximum amounts of antibodies in her colostrum to protect her pups if she is vaccinated at this time. If you vaccinate your own dogs, never vaccinate a bitch less than one month before breeding her because many vaccines contain modified-live viruses. If there is a break in the vaccine and the viruses are infective, they may affect the embryos adversely. Individual vaccinations may be staggered (that is, several weeks may be placed between each individual injection). If vaccinations are staggered, a bitch's vaccination schedule should be started two to three months before breeding her.

This is also a good time to have blood samples drawn. The results of a brucellosis test may not be back in time to breed a bitch if a blood sample is not taken until proestrus. Every bitch should also be tested annually for heartworm. If the bitch cycles irregularly or if her breed has a problem with hypothyroidism, a sample of blood should be drawn to evaluate thyroid levels. If her breed is predisposed to one of the blood dyscrasias, such as von Willebrand's disease, a sample of blood should also be drawn to evaluate blood clotting. Since many of these tests must be sent to far-off laboratories, results may not be available for some time.

Never underestimate the value of a general physical examination; underneath each veterinarian lies an unprofessed judge.

BRUCELLOSIS TESTING

Brucellosis is an infectious disease usually evidenced by reproductive failure. It often causes late-term abortion in bitches and testicular abnormalities in males. Systemic signs of disease are not usually apparent.

Brucellosis is highly contagious and is usually caused by a bacteria known as *Brucella canis*. This organism is transmitted by infected urine, semen, vaginal secretions and aborted fetuses. It can also infect people and, therefore, poses a public health threat. *Brucella canis* lives within cells. This makes it very difficult to treat infections. Simple antibiotic therapy will not cure most infected dogs and so they remain carriers for many years.

All breeding stock should be periodically tested for brucellosis. Active stud dogs should be tested every six months. Brood bitches should be tested within one month of breeding. Some veterinarians believe that bitches should be tested twice before each breeding: one month and then two weeks before. A negative brucellosis test result should always be obtained before purchasing a new brood bitch or stud dog.

There are two different tests commonly used to test for brucellosis. Please refer to the flow sheet in Figure 8-1. I believe that all dogs should be tested with the slide agglutination test as a routine screening procedure. The reason that I insist on using the slide test is that a negative truly means that the dog is free from infection. Sometimes dogs that are free from infection will test positive on the slide test. This may be the result of an infection with kennel cough. If a dog tests positive on the slide test, there is no reason to panic. Simply follow through with a tube agglutination test. If a dog tests positive on the slide test and negative on the tube test, the dog is probably free from infection. If this situation arises, consult with your veterinarian on a third test, the AGID (agar gel immunodiffusion test).

Many dogs that actually are infected will test negative on the tube test. That is why I do not recommend it as a screening test.

negative ○

slide test   negative ○

positive—tube test

positive △

○ = Dog is truly free from infection with brucella
△ = Dog is infected with brucella—perform AGID

Figure 8-1   Testing for Brucellosis

TIMING

Ask anyone knowledgeable about breeding dogs and they will say that the most common reason people fail to get dogs bred is improper timing. Thus, it is important to understand the normal sequence of events in a bitch's estrous or "heat" cycle.

Normal Estrous Cycle

The normal estrous cycle of the bitch is comprised of a set of physical events and a set of hormonal events. Although the physical and hormonal events occur concurrently, they are easier to understand when discussed separately.

Physical Events

The normal estrous cycle of the bitch is indeed cyclic, but it can be broken down into four distinct stages: proestrus, estrus, diestrus and anestrus (see Table 8-1). Please note the difference in spelling between "estrous" (an adjective applied to the entire cycle) and "estrus" (a stage within the entire cycle).

The cycle begins with proestrus, which usually lasts nine days but can range from three to seventeen days in length. Most bitches in a normal proestrus stage will have a bloody vaginal discharge. The vulva gradually begins to swell at this stage.

The next stage for a bitch to enter is estrus, or "standing heat." Estrus, like proestrus, normally lasts nine days but may range from three to twenty-one days in length. Some bitches continue to have a bloody vaginal discharge. Most bitches, however, have a gradual change in the vaginal discharge from bloody to straw colored. The vulva becomes enlarged and softened. Most bitches in estrus are receptive to males. They are extremely flirtatious and will stand for the male to mount them. Hence, the term "standing heat." Classically, bitches in standing heat will pull their tails off to one side of their backs. This is termed *flagging*. There is great variability between bitches with respect to flagging, and thus it is not an accurate sign of estrus in many bitches.

Diestrus is the next stage of the estrous cycle, and it usually lasts approximately sixty days. Once a bitch enters diestrus, she will usually refuse a male's advances.

Anestrus is the final stage of the estrous cycle and is the period of sexual inactivity. Its length is variable between bitches but is fairly constant for any given bitch. Some breeds of dogs, such as the Basenji and the Dingo, have exceptionally long periods of anestrus; hence, they only cycle once a year.

Table 8-1
Normal Estrous Cycle

Stage	Duration (range)	Signs
Proestrus	9 days (3 to 17)	Vaginal discharge
Estrus	9 days (3 to 21)	Receptive to males, swollen vulva, variable discharge
Diestrus	60 days (50 to 80)	Refuses male
Anestrus	150 to 250 days	Sexually inactive

Hormonal Events

During estrus, several important hormonal events take place. In order to understand these hormonal events, a study of some basic endocrinology is needed.

There are three hormones vital to the estrous cycle of the bitch: estrogen, luteinizing hormone (LH) and progesterone. Estrogen is the female hormone that initiates the estrous cycle. LH is the female hormone responsible for causing ovulation. Progesterone is the female hormone responsible for maintaining pregnancy.

The level of circulating estrogen begins to rise about one month before proestrus begins. Estrogen peaks and falls late in proestrus.

When estrogen peaks and falls, progesterone begins to rise. The level of progesterone gradually continues to rise throughout estrus. It maintains a plateau throughout estrus and falls precipitously when labor or false pregnancy ensues.

LH has a sudden, sharp peak when estrogen falls and progesterone rises. This burst of LH is known as the LH surge, and it usually occurs during estrus when the level of progesterone reaches a minimum concentration of 2 ng/ml.

In turn, the LH surge stimulates the ovaries to release eggs. This release of eggs is known as ovulation and will occur two to three days after the LH surge.

Eggs released from the ovaries must mature for two to three days before they can be fertilized by sperm. Fertilization occurs within the uterus. Once fertilized, the eggs remain free within the uterus until implantation begins. When the fertilized eggs implant, they burrow into the wall of the uterus. Implantation usually occurs about eighteen days after fertilization.

The level of progesterone must remain elevated in order to maintain a normal pregnancy.

Unfortunately, there is no consistent correlation between physical and hormonal events of the bitch's cycle. Most bitches will, however, enter estrus when the LH surge occurs and will ovulate sometime during estrus.

It is important to remember that few events in the bitch's cycle are fixed in length. The two fixed events are that ovulation will occur two to three days after the LH surge and that ovulated eggs will be ready for fertilization two to three days after ovulation. In summary, the hormonal events in the bitch's estrous cycle are as follows:

- Estrogen rises and falls
- Progesterone gradually rises above 2 ng/ml
- LH surge
- Ovulation (two to three days later)
- Fertilization of mature eggs (two to three days later)
- Progesterone drops (two months later)
- Whelping or false pregnancy

Objective Evaluation of Events

There are three ways to objectively evaluate the stages of a bitch's estrous cycle: progesterone assays, vaginal cytology and vaginal inspection.

Progesterone Assays

The amount of progesterone in a bitch's bloodstream can be measured readily. The test most commonly used to obtain rapid results is an in-house test that can easily be performed in almost any veterinary clinic. It is a simple test to perform, but it does not give an absolute value for the amount of progesterone. Rather, it gives results that fit into three possible ranges. The ranges are 0 to 1 ng/ml (corresponding to a blue color), approximately 2 ng/ml (corresponding to a light blue color) and >5 ng/ml (corresponding to a white color).

During proestrus, progesterone will remain low and will be between 0 and 1 ng/ml (blue).

The LH surge coincides with a sudden, abrupt rise to approximately 2 ng/ml (light blue). Identifying the day that the LH surge occurs has several important uses. One use is to accurately determine when to breed an individual bitch. In order to breed a bitch when her eggs are ready to be fertilized, she should be bred four to six days after the LH surge. Another use is to determine whether or not ovulation has occurred. An occasional bitch is infertile because she does not ovulate. If this is the case for an infertile bitch, a hormone injection may stimulate her to ovulate.

After the LH surge, progesterone normally rises rapidly to a value greater than 5 ng/ml (white) and remains high throughout pregnancy. Recording the changes in progesterone levels in a bitch's blood can be useful for solving fertility problems. Some bitches do not sustain a level of progesterone high enough to maintain pregnancy. If this is the case for an infertile bitch, she may be given supplemental progesterone in order to allow her to maintain a normal pregnancy and whelp a healthy litter.

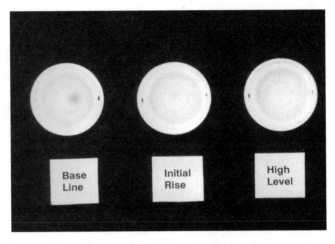

Shown here are the materials involved in a progesterone assay. This is a valuable aid in timing breedings.

International Canine Genetics, Inc.

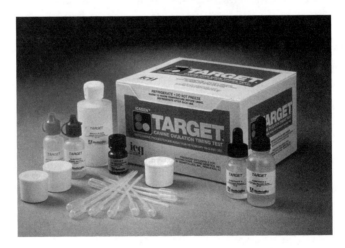

Vaginal Cytology

The particular types of cells found in a bitch's vagina during the estrous cycle can be examined and used to pinpoint the current stage of the estrous cycle.

Cells are collected from a bitch's vagina by inserting a long, moistened cotton swab into the vagina. Saline or plain tap water should be used to moisten the swab and cells should be collected from the farthest reaches of the vagina. The swab is then rolled onto a plain glass microscope slide. Cells can be stained for easier viewing with any one of a number of stains. Each veterinarian seems to have a preferred stain to use for vaginal cytology. Finally, the stained slide is examined under a microscope.

Two basic types of cells will be collected from the bitch's vaginal lining. One is a large, round cell that has a large center, or nucleus. It is called a noncornified cell. The second cell type has linear edges and either a very small, dark nucleus or no nucleus at all. It is called a cornified or squamous cell. Other types of cells that may be collected from the vagina are red blood cells (RBC) and white blood cells (WBC). RBC are commonly seen with proestral bleeding. WBC may occasionally be seen in a normal vaginal smear. Excessive numbers of WBC at certain stages may indicate that the bitch has a vaginal or uterine infection.

Hormonal changes mandate which type of cell will predominate. Hence, the stage of the estrous cycle is determined by comparing the relative numbers of cornified versus noncornified cells.

Early in proestrus, all the cells will be noncornified. As proestrus progresses, more cornified cells will be seen.

Estrus commences when more than 90 percent of the cells seen on the slide are cornified. Please note that the date of ovulation cannot be predicted through the use of vaginal smears. This is because ovulation may occur at any time during the estrus stage, and its date varies dramatically between bitches.

Vaginal smears can be used to identify the first day of diestrus, which may or may not coincide exactly with the first day that the bitch refuses the male. Diestrus begins when more than 50 percent of the cells seen on the slide revert to being noncornified. The first day of diestrus (as evidenced by a vaginal smear) can be used to accurately predict a whelping date. Whelping occurs fifty-seven days after the first day of diestrus.

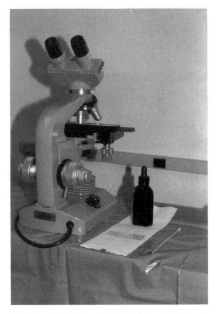

To perform vaginal smears a microscope, a sterile slide, staining material and a supply of long cotton swabs are essential items.

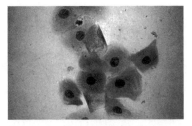

A vaginal smear from a bitch in proestrus showing primarily noncornified cells, which may be described as being round, with large nuclei.   *International Canine Genetics, Inc.*

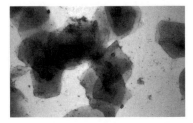

A vaginal smear from a bitch in estrus showing primarily cornified cells. These are described as angular cells with small or absent nuclei.
International Canine Genetics, Inc.

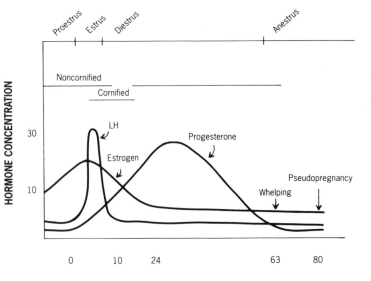

Hormonal changes of the estrus cycle. After T.N. Nett and P.N. Olsen "Peripheral Concentrations of Reproductive Hormones, Estrual Activity and Changes in Vaginal Epithelial Cells during the Estrus Cycle of the Bitch. In S.J. Ettinger, ed. *Textbook of Veterinary Internal Medicine*, 2nd ed., Vol. II (Philadelphia: W.B. Saunders, 1983).

Vaginal Inspection

Some veterinarians who specialize in reproduction have become adept at staging a bitch's estrous cycle simply by visually inspecting a bitch's vagina. A proctoscope must be inserted into the bitch's vagina, and a good light source is needed to adequately see the vaginal lining. In general, as estrous progresses, the lining becomes thick and heavily folded.

Subjective Evaluation of Events

Nothing in life replaces knowledge gained through experience. If you are a novice breeder, consult the person who bred your bitch. Some breeds, and even some lines within a given breed, have peculiar idiosyncrasies. Only experience will pinpoint these idiosyncrasies. Learn as much as possible about your breed and your particular line. It will save you much grief and prevent you from having to learn many things the hard way.

When to Breed?

Since improper timing of breeding is the most important reason for breeding failures, asking exactly when to breed becomes an all-important question. Unfortunately, there is no simple, straightforward answer to that question.

If the bitch is a maiden, meaning that she has never been bred before, you can:

1. Breed her every other day for a total of three matings, starting on her first day of standing heat. If she is still in standing heat on day twenty-one of her estrous cycle, she should be bred on an every-other-day schedule until she refuses the male. If at all possible, an experienced, reliable stud dog should be used for maiden bitches. The sense of smell of most studs is far superior to and more accurate than any laboratory test. Keep in mind that a reliable stud is one that knows when to breed and shows it. A reliable stud is not so maniacal that he must be tranquilized throughout most of an estrous cycle.
2. Have samples of blood collected every other day throughout

proestrus until the day of the LH surge. If you can pinpoint the day that the LH surge occurs, begin breeding her four days after the LH surge. This should coincide with the day of maturation. Some research studies indicate that you can maximize litter size by breeding on the day that the eggs are mature. Again, breed her every other day for a total of three matings. Most veterinarians will take swab samples for vaginal cytology at the same time that blood samples are taken for progesterone assays. If there is a discrepancy between the vaginal cytology and the progesterone assay, rely on the progesterone assay.

If the bitch is not a maiden, you can:

1. Review records of previous breedings and whelpings. If she has been bred before but has failed to whelp a litter, review Chapter 14.
2. If she has been bred before and has whelped a litter, get out all your records, a whelping calendar and a notebook. Be honest with yourself. How likely were you to have noticed the very first day of proestrus? If there is any doubt in your mind, assume that you may have missed that first day. If there is a discrepancy between the length of seasons, this may be the explanation.

Jot down any whelping dates and count back sixty-three days from the day of whelping with the help of a whelping calendar. This day—sixty-three days before whelping—is the day of ovulation. For example, if a bitch was bred on the tenth day of estrus and whelped sixty-three days later, she was bred on the day of ovulation. Provided that her seasons are consistent, she should be bred on the twelfth day of her season the next time.

Remember, if you breed two days after ovulation, you may maximize litter size. If there is a discrepancy between litter sizes, this may be the explanation.

Review all your notes and make decisions regarding when to breed her with all these facts in mind.

If you are going to ship a bitch:

1. Ship her as soon as you notice proestrus. This will give the bitch plenty of time to acclimate to a new kennel environment before she is bred.

2. Do everything you can to minimize the stress associated with shipping. Stress is known to cause infertility. It may preclude implantation or cause fetal resorption.

If the bitch is not already accustomed to spending time in a travel crate, acclimate her long before her anticipated shipping. If she has not been well socialized, take her to visit as many friends as you can muster. Make these occasions exceptionally enjoyable for her. Be careful, though, not to expose her unnecessarily to parasites or infectious diseases too soon before shipping.

Have the stud dog owner agree to feed your bitch the same feed that she receives at home. If you have well water and the stud dog owner does not, pay the stud dog owner to buy her spring water. In short, try to make her new environment as similar to her home environment as possible. Attention to detail pays. A conscientious stud dog owner will be as anxious to see her successfully bred as you are. Not only are most stud owners hesitant to have their dogs "miss" and risk rumors of infertility, but they also are usually anxious to avoid a repeat visit. If the stud dog owner is reluctant to offer you a repeat service, go elsewhere. No dog's sperm is that valuable, and you should question the motives of such an owner.

Preventing Estrus

People may wish to keep their bitches from entering estrus for a number of different reasons. Bitches cannot compete in obedience and field events while in estrus. Some bitches blow their coats after they've been in season. And all bitches disrupt tranquil homes when they enter estrus.

Two drugs are currently used to prevent bitches from entering estrus. They are megestrol acetate (which goes by the trade name of Ovaban) and mibolerone (known as Cheque Drops).

Ovaban has no adverse effect on subsequent fertility of the bitch, according to the manufacturer. It cannot, however, be used on a bitch's first season or for more than two consecutive seasons. Once Ovaban has been discontinued, there is a great variability in the amount of time that passes before the bitch reenters an estrous cycle. With long-term use, diabetes and/or breast cancer may result.

Cheque Drops (mibolerone) is not recommended for breeding bitches even though subsequent fertility seems to be good. It must be started at least thirty days before the next season is due. Like

Ovaban, it cannot be used in a bitch's first season, and there is a great variability as to when a bitch will reenter estrus after Cheque Drops has been discontinued. German Shepherd Dogs require a larger dose than other breeds. If given to pregnant bitches, it causes defects in the urogenital tracts of puppies. It is an androgenic steroid and so all puppies will appear to be male. The drug has been shown to cause skin problems, liver disease, thyroid dysfunction and clitoral enlargement.

Some breeders successfully use chlorophyll tablets to mask the scent of a bitch in season. Chlorophyll in no way alters the actual season.

NATURAL BREEDINGS

"Natural breedings" should be anything but natural. Ideally, prospective mates should be selected, the settings should be contrived and records should be kept meticulously.

The setting is all-important and should be quiet. No other dogs and only two human handlers should be present. The footing should be secure for the male. If the male is too short for the bitch, he may need to have a platform built for him. A virgin bitch usually should be muzzled. A grooming table often helps when breeding toy breeds of dogs. If no assistant is available, the bitch should be fitted with a buckle collar and a leash. The leash can then be tied to chain-link fencing or a doorknob, whichever is more convenient.

The bitch should be showing behavioral signs of estrus—that is, she should be flirtatious with the male and she should stand motionless so that the male may mount her.

The male should show a distinct interest in the bitch. He should lick her vulva and attempt to mount her. He may choose not to mount her if she is either not ready or not willing. If the male appears uninterested and the bitch appears willing, the pair should be separated for twenty-four hours. Physical separation may sharpen his interest in her. If it is impossible to wait twenty-four hours, an artificial insemination (AI) can sometimes be performed. Unfortunately, some males cannot be collected if they ascertain that the bitch is not yet ready to be bred.

Inexperienced males sometimes fail to penetrate the bitch. If the stud is comfortable with handling and if he has not reached a full erection, his penis may be gently guided into the vulva. If he

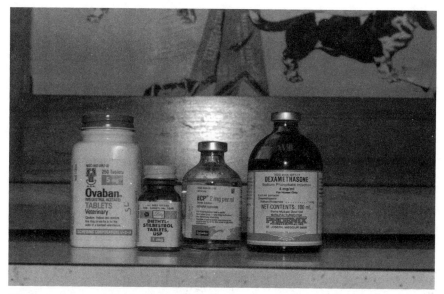

There are a number of different drugs that are capable of preventing estrus or negating an accidental, unwanted mating.

The Irish Setter Kalliber's Colt Forty-Five sired the first puppy from frozen semen breeding registered by the American Kennel Club.   *Rizzo*

87

already has a full erection, he cannot obtain an inside tie and he should be rested until his penis is no longer erect.

Stud dogs can be used every other day without harming their fertility. Daily use, however, will decrease semen quality after about one week.

Individual bitches should be bred every forty-eight hours until they refuse to stand for breeding. Two or three breedings are usually adequate. As previously mentioned, breeding should resume if the bitch is still standing on day twenty-one.

The bitch should be discouraged from urinating for fifteen minutes after the breeding. The stud dog should never be put away until his erection has completely subsided. When the erection subsides, the penis should slip back into the prepuce. (The prepuce is the skin that covers the nonerect penis.) If the penis is exposed for long periods of time, it may suffer irreparable damage.

ARTIFICIAL INSEMINATION

Artificial insemination is breeding without mating. Semen is collected from a male and artificially inseminated into the female. There are three types of semen used in artificial insemination: fresh semen, extended semen and frozen semen.

With fresh-semen artificial inseminations, semen is collected from the stud and immediately inseminated into the bitch. This procedure is used for a number of reasons. Physical problems with a bitch that could preclude a natural breeding include vaginal strictures and oversized stature. Mental problems might include an aggressive attitude toward a valuable stud and a determined will to choose her own mate. Some males will have a physical or mental problem that precludes a natural mating. For example, he may be too old and arthritic to mount a female, or he may be inexperienced and not know what to do. With many virginal studs, one experience with fresh AI will miraculously teach him what to do.

Extended semen AI is just now coming into its own. In this case, semen is collected from a male in one geographical region, mixed with a semen extender to prolong the life of the sperm and shipped to the bitch in another geographical location to be used as soon as possible. When using extended semen AI, timing is of the utmost importance for two reasons. First, the procedure is not inexpensive and usually only two samples will be collected. Second, extended semen has a lifespan of only two or three days. Fresh semen, on the other hand, is reported to live within a bitch's reproductive tract from seven to eleven days after ejaculation.

Frozen semen AI is the procedure used least often. One of the greatest problems with canine frozen semen is that the sperm seem to have decreased motility. As a result, conception rates are greatly enchanced by inseminating frozen semen directly into the uterus of bitches rather than inseminating into the vagina. This requires general anesthesia and surgical exploration to find the uterus. Although this is very stressful for the bitch, conception rates for intrauterine insemination have been as high as 75 percent.

Some ethical issues are raised from the use of frozen semen and will need to be addressed when the technique becomes more widely available. Obviously, frozen semen has its greatest value in maintaining the gene pool from great stud dogs that are deceased. The biggest issue raised will be whether or not we will unwisely use a limited number of widely acclaimed stud dogs and thereby markedly limit the available gene pool for any given breed. The Thoroughbred Racing Association has a firm stance against artificial insemination of any kind and does not allow registration of foals that result from AI breedings. The American Kennel Club, on the other hand, allows a fairly liberal use of AI. Please consult the AKC before using AI to find out exactly what their current position on this issue is.

It is important to note that those who operate businesses involved with canine frozen semen strongly advocate that semen be collected from stud dogs while they are still young. It is human nature to look at veteran stud dogs and wonder whether or not they will live long enough to sire that one last litter. The future is better served by collecting and freezing semen from stud dogs while they are still young and virile.

Artificial insemination is a relatively simple, two-step procedure. The first step is to collect the semen from the stud dog. The second is to inseminate the semen into the receptive bitch.

If you plan to perform your own AIs, have a veterinarian or a knowledgeable breeder teach you how to go about performing the AI. Few supplies are needed for fresh semen AI. (Supplies for extended and frozen semen AI are provided by the companies that oversee these matings.) You will need to purchase a tube to collect semen into, a sleeve to fit between the dog's penis and the collection tube, a syringe to draw up the semen from the collection tube and a pipette to insert the semen into the bitch's vagina. Be certain to purchase supplies from a reputable dealer, as certain chemicals will kill sperm cells on contact. And don't forget to consult the AKC to find out what restrictions they may have regarding registration of puppies resulting from AI matings.

A teaser bitch is often needed to collect semen from the stud dog. The bitch may actually be in estrus or she may be in anestrus. If the teaser bitch is not in estrus, she will need to smell as though she were. This can be accomplished with a little preparation. Anytime a bitch in estrus is available, a tissue should be smeared against her vulva. The tissue can then be wrapped well and stored in a freezer until needed. Most of these tissues have a lifespan of one to three months when frozen. When needed, these tissues can be removed from the freezer, unwrapped and tied to the tail of an anestrus teaser bitch.

The stud and the teaser bitch should be introduced as any other breeding pair. If the teaser bitch is in anestrus, she should be muzzled. When the stud shows interest in the teaser bitch, the sleeve is placed on his penis. Then the male is ejaculated. The actual art of collecting from a stud dog is best illustrated by an experienced hand. Before the stud is placed in his kennel run or crate, his penis should be carefully inspected to ensure that the erection has subsided and that the penis is back in the prepuce.

Three different fractions of semen will be ejaculated by the male. Some people inseminate all three into the receptive bitch. Most people dispense with the last fraction and only inseminate the first and second fractions. The second, sperm-rich fraction will be milky white in color. If a veterinarian is inseminating for you, he or she will be able to take a semen sample and examine it under a microscope to evaluate the quality and quantity of sperm.

It is very important to keep the sperm warm between collection and insemination. Most people accomplish this by holding the collection tube in their hands and gently rolling it.

To inseminate the bitch, a pipette is gently placed into her vagina. Exact positioning is best done by an experienced inseminator in order to avoid harming the bitch's reproductive tract and to ensure proper placement. Semen is drawn up into the syringe, the syringe is attached to the pipette and its contents are injected into the bitch's

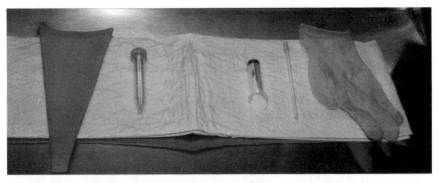

To perform artificial insemination one requires (from left) a sleeve that is placed over the dog's sheath and a collection tube, syringe, pipette and glove.

To collect semen, it is first necessary to arouse the stud dog. Obviously the "teaser" bitch need not be of the same breed.

Semen collection. *International Canine Genetics, Inc.*

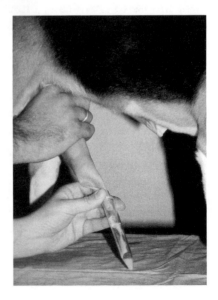

vagina through the pipette. To ensure that all the semen has been propelled into the vagina, air is injected into the pipette before it is removed from the bitch. After the pipette is withdrawn, a gloved finger should be placed into the vagina and used to gently feather the top of the bitch's vagina. This act of feathering is believed to stimulate uterine contractions and help propel the sperm toward the eggs. While the vagina is being feathered, the bitch's rear should be elevated and held above her front end for five to fifteen minutes. She should not be allowed to urinate for an additional fifteen minutes. No lubricant other than plain tap water should be used on the gloved finger, as many lubricants are spermicidal.

MISMATING

Mismating occurs when bitch A is bred to stud dog B when bitch A was either not to be bred this season or not to be bred to stud dog B.

Whatever the reason, a mismating occasionally occurs. There are three viable options to pursue if a bitch is mismated: nothing can be done, the bitch can be spayed or drugs can be used to interfere with the unwanted pregnancy. I usually recommend simply letting nature take her course. The mating may not even take. Obviously, few breeders will opt to spay their bitch. Some people, however, will choose to chemically interfere with the pregnancy, even though drugs used for this purpose have shortcomings and possible undesirable side effects.

Two drugs are commonly used for mismatings. They are estradiol cyptionate (ECP) and diethylstilbestrol (DES). ECP is an injectable, long-lasting estrogen. Only one injection can be given in one heat cycle. (In other words, she cannot be caught again in that same heat cycle.) One possible side effect is a fatal suppression of the bitch's bone marrow. Another possible side effect is pyometra. Pyometra is an infected uterus, which is rarely cured without spaying the bitch. DES is another estrogen used to treat mismating. It can be given orally. It, too, can cause bone marrow suppression and pyometra. Both of these drugs must be given within forty-eight hours of the mismating in order to be effective. They tend to prolong estrus, and thus later matings may result in pregnancy. Additionally, they are not 100 percent effective.

A third drug may be used to treat mismatings. Dexamethasone

When handling teaser bitches, many handlers like to use a gauze muzzle for the safety of all concerned.

Commercial muzzles are also available for use on anestrus teaser bitches and may be preferable when handling bitches of larger breeds.

This large litter of English Springer Spaniel puppies is the result of artificial insemination.   *Zafian*

is an injectable steroid that may be given twice daily for ten consecutive days beginning thirty days after the mating in order to induce abortion. It is not widely used, for a number of reasons. Midterm abortion has serious risks for the bitch. Additionally, a series of twenty injections can be quite expensive. As with ECP and DES, this treatment is also less than 100 percent effective.

9

Pregnancy

SEVERAL ADVANCES have recently been made in the study of canine reproduction that can be quite useful in managing pregnancy. Presently, pregnancy can be reliably detected with a number of different techniques. A whelping date can now be accurately predicted for many bitches. New knowledge can also be used to greatly improve the care of pregnant bitches.

PREGNANCY DETECTION

Pregnancy detection serves two purposes. First, it serves to help solve many fertility problems. Problems may be uncovered in bitches that conceive that are different from the problems of those that do not conceive. Second, pregnancy detection serves to help decision making with respect to who should or should not be bred. If one bitch does not take, another bitch may be bred in her place, since most bitches cycle together.

Five methods are currently used to detect pregnancy in bitches: abdominal palpation, radiography, ultrasound, behavioral signs and a new biological test.

Abdominal Palpation

The word "palpate" means "to feel with one's hands." Many skilled veterinarians can reliably detect pregnancy by palpating a bitch's abdomen. Most veterinarians successfully palpate bitches between twenty-one and twenty-eight days of gestation. At this stage, the pregnant uterus feels like a string of pearls; each pearl represents an individual fetus. I prefer to palpate bitches twice—once at twenty-one and again at twenty-eight days. Often, I simply feel an enlarged uterus on the twenty-first day. By the twenty-eighth day, I can usually feel individual fetuses.

Palpation is an inexpensive method for pregnancy detection. It is also widely available. All that is required is a person skilled at palpation and a calm, cooperative bitch. I do not recommend that laymen palpate bitches; if the person palpating a bitch is too rough, the bitch may abort. Rather, I recommend that you find a veterinarian whom you are comfortable with to do palpations for you.

Palpation is not 100 percent reliable, and it can never be used to predict litter size, as many puppies may be hidden underneath the bitch's rib cage. Recently I palpated two puppies in the caudal abdomen of a German Shorthaired Pointer bitch. She also had four other puppies hidden underneath her ribs and went on to whelp six puppies.

Radiography

Radiography is another relatively inexpensive and widely available method of pregnancy detection. Radiographs, or X-rays, taken of bitches late in gestation will reveal fetal skeletons and, thus, can be used to detect pregnancy. Radiographs taken too early in a pregnancy will not detect fetuses. This is because fetal skeletons do not deposit enough calcium in their bones to be visible on an X-ray before the forty-second day of gestation. Radiographs taken too early in a pregnancy may also have adverse effects on developing fetuses. However, no ill effects are known to occur when radiographs are taken after the forty-second day.

Radiographs are not usually used merely to detect pregnancy. By the forty-second day of gestation, most breeders can tell whether a bitch is in whelp. Radiographs are usually taken to identify potential whelping problems. X-rays may reveal maternal pelvic fractures that would interfere with normal whelping. They will also often

Palpation is an inexpensive method to determine pregnancy in bitches. It cannot guarantee accuracy as to the number of puppies and is only as dependable as the skill of the person making the determination.

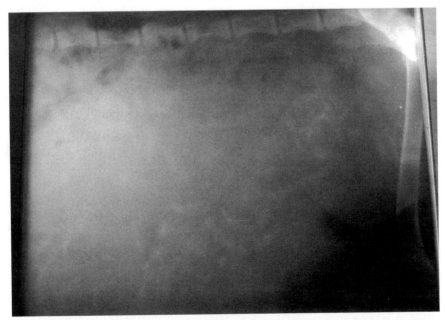

Radiograph of a bitch in whelp during the final third of her pregnancy.

reveal dead fetuses, abnormally large puppies or single-puppy litters. They cannot, however, be used to reliably judge exact litter sizes in large litters, as fetal skeletons overlap one another.

Ultrasound

Ultrasound is a technology that uses sound waves to produce images. An analogy can be made between medical ultrasound and the sonar used by submarines. A sound wave is produced and directed toward an object. When the wave hits a solid object, it is reflected and returns to the machine. The machine, in turn, reads the returned wave and interprets it. In the case of medical ultrasound, a visual image is usually produced. When ultrasound is used to detect pregnancy, some of the individual fetuses can be identified.

Ultrasound is a safe and reliable method of pregnancy detection. It causes no known adverse effects on developing fetuses. Although it is usually used to detect pregnancy after the thirty-second day, on many machines ultrasound can be used to reliably detect pregnancy as early as the eighteenth day. Some machines can identify fetal heartbeats and, thus, indicate whether or not the fetuses are alive.

Ultrasound does, however, have its shortcomings. It is, unfortunately, not widely available because the equipment needed to perform ultrasound is too expensive for most veterinarians to purchase. As with radiography, ultrasound cannot detect all fetuses in any given litter. Ultrasound, like abdominal palpation, can detect early pregnancies but cannot predict which pregnancies will be carried to term. One must keep in mind that many losses occur early in pregnancy. If ultrasound detects pregnancy in the early stages, this is no guarantee that the litter will be carried to term.

Behavioral Signs

Many nonpregnant bitches routinely go through pseudocyesis, or false pregnancy. The severity of signs can range widely. Some bitches display false pregnancy very dramatically. They may develop full milk production, strong nesting behavior and protective maternal aggression. Many of these bitches nurture and protect toys exactly as they would live puppies. These behavioral changes can be quite alarming to ignorant dog owners. Other bitches, however, display minimal signs of false pregnancy.

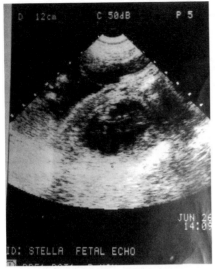
Ultrasound of a canine fetus.

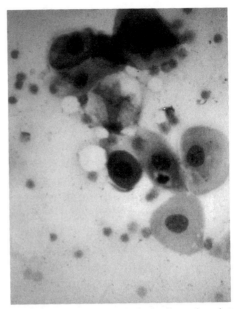
Vaginal smears can be used to pinpoint the first day of diestrus, which, in turn, can be used to predict the whelping date.
International Canine Genetics, Inc.

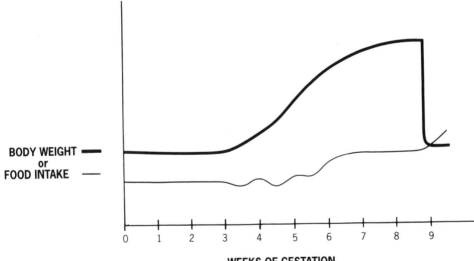

BODY WEIGHT ▬
or
FOOD INTAKE ▬

WEEKS OF GESTATION

Weight gain and food intake during pregnancy. After L.D. Lewis, M.L. Morris and M.S. Hand, "Body Weight and Food Intake during Gestation and Lactation in the Bitch." In L.D. Lewis, M.L. Morris and M.S. Hand, *Small Animal Clinical Nutrition*, 3rd ed. (Topeka: Mark Morris Associates, 1987).

Most animal behaviorists believe that pseudocyesis is a throwback to the natural behavior patterns of pack animals such as the wolf. In wild packs of wolves, only one male and only one female mate and reproduce. They produce one litter each year that is nurtured by the entire pack. Only the dominant bitch is truly pregnant. All the submissive bitches in a pack enter a pseudocyesis, produce milk and care for the dominant bitch's litter.

This theory explains much of the behavior we see in domestic dogs. Usually, all bitches in one kennel will go through estrus simultaneously or nearly so. One dominant bitch in the kennel often violently fends off the advances of males toward the other, submissive bitches. Submissive bitches, in turn, usually enter into false pregnancies. This natural behavior pattern makes it difficult to assess true pregnancy in domestic dogs; any nonpregnant bitch may exhibit any or all signs of pregnancy.

Most pregnant bitches will develop morning sickness three to four weeks after being bred. They are usually too nauseous to eat; if they do eat, they may vomit. Some bitches may develop a mucus plug about one month into the pregnancy. The mucus plug is a clear, gelatinous blob of tissue located in the vulva. Fortunately, few bitches in false pregnancies exhibit morning sickness or develop a mucus plug.

DETERMINING A WHELPING DATE

Although there are a number of ways to estimate a whelping date, the one way to accurately predict it is to determine the date of ovulation. *Whelping will invariably occur sixty-three days after ovulation.*

There are two ways to determine just when ovulation occurs. One way is to take blood samples and measure progesterone levels. If progesterone levels are measured throughout proestrus and early estrus, the LH peak will be identified. Ovulation occurs one to three days *after* the LH peak. Since ovulation occurs about two days after the LH peak, *whelping will occur about sixty-five days after the LH peak.*

A second, retrospective way to determine when ovulation occurs is to obtain vaginal smears. If vaginal smears are followed through the end of estrus, the first day of diestrus will be identified. Ovulation occurs five to seven days *before* the first day of diestrus.

Since ovulation occurs about six days before the first day of diestrus, *whelping will occur about fifty-seven days after the first day of diestrus*.

Therefore, normal gestation may last from fifty-seven to sixty-eight days from the first day of breeding. When a fifty-seven-day gestation occurs, the first breeding took place on the first day of diestrus, or six days after ovulation. When a sixty-eight-day gestation occurs, the first day of breeding occurred five days before ovulation.

Most people estimate a whelping date through the use of a whelping calendar. Such calendars list two dates on any given day. The first date listed is the first day of breeding. The second date is the estimated whelping date sixty-three days later. Obviously, *the whelping calendar will only be accurate if the first day of breeding occurs on the day of ovulation*.

Some people believe that a large litter size will induce bitches to whelp sooner. This is unlikely. It is more likely that when bitches are bred relatively late in their cycle, they are bred closer to the day of fertilization. As a result of breeding on the day of fertilization, the litter size will be maximized while the length of gestation will be concurrently shortened to approximately sixty-one days.

Regardless of the method used to estimate a whelping date, the bitch's rectal temperature should be monitored twice daily for one week before the expected whelping. When the bitch's rectal temperature drops one full degree and remains low on the following reading, she is due to whelp within twenty-four hours. The bitch's rectal temperature often drops to 99° F or less.

CARE OF THE PREGNANT BITCH

As discussed in the previous chapter, pregnant bitches should never be vaccinated with modified-live viral vaccines. Additionally, pregnant bitches should never be given any unnecessary medications. Keep in mind that vitamins may be considered medications. I have not had any problems with heartworm preventatives and give diethylcarbamazine daily to my pregnant bitches. Do not discontinue thyroid medications for truly hypothyroid bitches. Consult your veterinarian if you have any questions regarding a medication.

The bitch's weight and overall condition must be closely monitored during pregnancy. Provided that she is in good condition at the time of breeding, the pregnant bitch should maintain the same

WHELPING CALENDAR

Find the month and date on which your bitch was bred in one of the left-hand columns. Directly opposite that date, in the right-hand column, is her expected date of whelping, bearing in mind that 61 days is as common as 63.

Date bred (Jan)	Date due to whelp (Mar)	Date bred (Feb)	Date due to whelp (Apr)	Date bred (Mar)	Date due to whelp (May)	Date bred (Apr)	Date due to whelp (Jun)	Date bred (May)	Date due to whelp (Jul)	Date bred (Jun)	Date due to whelp (Aug)	Date bred (Jul)	Date due to whelp (Sep)	Date bred (Aug)	Date due to whelp (Oct)	Date bred (Sep)	Date due to whelp (Nov)	Date bred (Oct)	Date due to whelp (Dec)	Date bred (Nov)	Date due to whelp (Jan)	Date bred (Dec)	Date due to whelp (Feb)
1	5	1	5	1	3	1	3	1	3	1	3	1	2	1	3	1	3	1	3	1	3	1	2
2	6	2	6	2	4	2	4	2	4	2	4	2	3	2	4	2	4	2	4	2	4	2	3
3	7	3	7	3	5	3	5	3	5	3	5	3	4	3	5	3	5	3	5	3	5	3	4
4	8	4	8	4	6	4	6	4	6	4	6	4	5	4	6	4	6	4	6	4	6	4	5
5	9	5	9	5	7	5	7	5	7	5	7	5	6	5	7	5	7	5	7	5	7	5	6
6	10	6	10	6	8	6	8	6	8	6	8	6	7	6	8	6	8	6	8	6	8	6	7
7	11	7	11	7	9	7	9	7	9	7	9	7	8	7	9	7	9	7	9	7	9	7	8
8	12	8	12	8	10	8	10	8	10	8	10	8	9	8	10	8	10	8	10	8	10	8	9
9	13	9	13	9	11	9	11	9	11	9	11	9	10	9	11	9	11	9	11	9	11	9	10
10	14	10	14	10	12	10	12	10	12	10	12	10	11	10	12	10	12	10	12	10	12	10	11
11	15	11	15	11	13	11	13	11	13	11	13	11	12	11	13	11	13	11	13	11	13	11	12
12	16	12	16	12	14	12	14	12	14	12	14	12	13	12	14	12	14	12	14	12	14	12	13
13	17	13	17	13	15	13	15	13	15	13	15	13	14	13	15	13	15	13	15	13	15	13	14
14	18	14	18	14	16	14	16	14	16	14	16	14	15	14	16	14	16	14	16	14	16	14	15
15	19	15	19	15	17	15	17	15	17	15	17	15	16	15	17	15	17	15	17	15	17	15	16
16	20	16	20	16	18	16	18	16	18	16	18	16	17	16	18	16	18	16	18	16	18	16	17
17	21	17	21	17	19	17	19	17	19	17	19	17	18	17	19	17	19	17	19	17	19	17	18
18	22	18	22	18	20	18	20	18	20	18	20	18	19	18	20	18	20	18	20	18	20	18	19
19	23	19	23	19	21	19	21	19	21	19	21	19	20	19	21	19	21	19	21	19	21	19	20
20	24	20	24	20	22	20	22	20	22	20	22	20	21	20	22	20	22	20	22	20	22	20	21
21	25	21	25	21	23	21	23	21	23	21	23	21	22	21	23	21	23	21	23	21	23	21	22
22	26	22	26	22	24	22	24	22	24	22	24	22	23	22	24	22	24	22	24	22	24	22	23
23	27	23	27	23	25	23	25	23	25	23	25	23	24	23	25	23	25	23	25	23	25	23	24
24	28	24	28	24	26	24	26	24	26	24	26	24	25	24	26	24	26	24	26	24	26	24	25
25	29	25	29	25	27	25	27	25	27	25	27	25	26	25	27	25	27	25	27	25	27	25	26
26	30	26	30	26	28	26	28	26	28	26	28	26	27	26	28	26	28	26	28	26	28	26	27
27	31 (Apr.)	27	1 (May)	27	29	27	29	27	29	27	29	27	28	27	29	27	29	27	29	27	29	27	28
28	1	28	2	28	30	28	30 (July)	28	30	28	30	28	29	28	30	28	30 (Dec.)	28	30	28	30	28	1 (Mar.)
29	2			29	31 (June)	29	1	29	31 (Aug.)	29	31 (Sep.)	29	30 (Oct.)	29	31 (Nov.)	29	1	29	31 (Jan.)	29	31 (Feb.)	29	2
30	3			30	1	30	2	30	1	30	1	30	1	30	1	30	2	30	1	30	1	30	3
31	4			31	2			31	2			31	2	31	2			31	2			31	4

weight throughout the first four weeks of gestation. Normal bitches will have small fluctuations in body weight during this time because they tend to have morning sickness and often are finicky eaters. After the fourth week of pregnancy, the bitch should steadily gain weight. How much she gains will depend on her size and the size of the litter. In general she can be expected to gain between 15 and 25 percent of her normal body weight. Be certain to objectively and subjectively monitor her weight weekly. Record her weight on a calendar and note her overall condition.

Overweight bitches will appear thick across the top of the loin and will have a more difficult time whelping. They tend to have fat puppies, and fat puppies are more difficult to deliver. Thus, do not allow the bitch to become too fat.

Malnourished bitches deliver puppies that lack sufficient stores of energy and such bitches also provide less milk to their nursing puppies. Underweight bitches will have a prominent backbone. If you suspect that your bitch may be malnourished, consult your veterinarian before breeding her. Your veterinarian can measure the bitch's red blood cell count and blood protein levels to look for an anemia or a protein deficiency. Force feeding during pregnancy should not become necessary if a premium puppy ration is being fed.

Bitches should be fed a premium-quality, puppy-ration dog food throughout pregnancy. Pregnant bitches, like puppies, cannot physically fill their stomachs full enough to obtain adequate nutrition from many other types of foods. Continue feeding puppy food throughout pregnancy and lactation. Pregnant bitches need one and one-quarter to two times their normal volume of food beginning with the fourth week of gestation. Lactating bitches often need three times the normal volume of food while nursing large litters. To help with weaning, begin to cut back on the volume of food fed to the dam and begin to introduce puppies to the food pan at about three weeks of age. It will be convenient to then gradually wean puppies with the same premium puppy food.

Some bitches develop eclampsia, or "milk fever," shortly before, during or after whelping. Signs of eclampsia include tremors, staggering, convulsions and/or fever. They are caused by hypocalcemia—low blood levels of calcium. The hypocalcemia, in turn, is due to the fact that the bitch must provide much calcium to the developing fetal skeletons or to the milk of the nursing puppies. It is seen most often in Toy breeds but may occur in any breed of dog.

Some veterinarians prefer to give bitches with a prior history of eclampsia supplemental calcium during pregnancy. Other veterinarians feel that this may actually be detrimental. Feeding puppy food, which is higher in calcium than adult rations, may be all that is needed to prevent eclampsia. Never supplement the diet of a pregnant bitch without the advice of your veterinarian. If you anticipate a problem, have your veterinarian draw a blood sample during the last trimester to check the bitch's blood calcium level.

Other bitches develop hypoglycemia, or low blood sugar, during pregnancy. Likewise, if you anticipate a problem, have your veterinarian draw a blood sample late in gestation to check the bitch's blood sugar level.

Allow a pregnant bitch to exercise lightly. A bitch with poor muscle tone will have a more difficult time whelping. Do not, however, allow her to roughhouse with other dogs or jump heights.

Check the bitch's vulva daily for signs of vaginal discharge. Most vaginal discharges during pregnancy indicate an impending problem. Your veterinarian should be contacted immediately if you detect a discharge.

Record the pregnant bitch's rectal temperature twice daily during her last week of pregnancy. Consult your veterinarian if her temperature rises above 103° F and prepare for the impending whelping if it drops below 99° F.

Confine the bitch to your premises during her pregnancy and prohibit the entrance of new dogs or dogs currently attending shows. This will prevent her from contracting new parasites or other infectious agents. All in all, let common sense prevail in caring for a pregnant bitch.

10

Whelping

MANY HOURS OF PREPARATION are needed for a successful whelping. All supplies that might become needed should be readied well in advance of the expected due date. A knowledgeable midwife must be available to assist in the delivery of the puppies. Any possible sign of a problem must be recognized and dealt with effectively and without delay.

WHELPING PREPARATIONS

The following supplies should be secured long before the anticipated whelping date:

- Whelping box with secure flooring material
- Heat lamp
- Clock
- Baby or food scale
- Note pad with pen
- Heating pad
- Cardboard box large enough for the newborns
- Lots of clean towels
- Sterile surgical gloves

- Hemostat
- Pair of scissors
- Dental floss
- 3% hydrogen peroxide
- Rectal thermometer
- Milk replacer
- Nursing kit

Whelping Box

The whelping box should be placed in a quiet, reclusive spot. Accustom the bitch to the box one or two weeks before the anticipated delivery if she is unfamiliar with the whelping room. The room selected should have a separate thermostat or portable heating unit and must be free from drafts.

The size of the whelping box will obviously depend on the size of the bitch. In general, the box should be one and a half times the length of the dam. Consult the person who bred your bitch for helpful hints.

Most whelping boxes are constructed of wood. They have four sides and each side has an inner railing. The inner railing serves to protect the puppies from being suffocated by the dam. Whelping boxes constructed with a solid wooden floor are often difficult to clean thoroughly. A plastic tarp may be used instead of a solid wooden floor. In either case, flooring material will be needed. Since it is disposable, plain newsprint may be used for the actual whelping. Something other than newsprint is needed later to give developing puppies secure footing. Puppies raised on slippery flooring may develop into "swimmer puppies"—puppies that are flattened and cannot ambulate adequately. A variety of materials may be used, such as blankets, fake sheepskin or indoor/outdoor carpeting. Whatever material is chosen, it should be machine washable. Sometimes it is most convenient to take soiled flooring to the local Laundromat.

Improvisations often make adequate whelping boxes. Children's inflatable swimming pools or solid, plastic wading pools may be used; these can be hosed for easy cleaning. Some toy breeders simply use large cardboard boxes. Cardboard boxes are readily and cheaply replaced. All in all, however, the tried-and-true wooden box with inner railings is probably best.

Whelping boxes constructed with adjustable side heights are very useful. They allow the bitch to exit and enter the box without

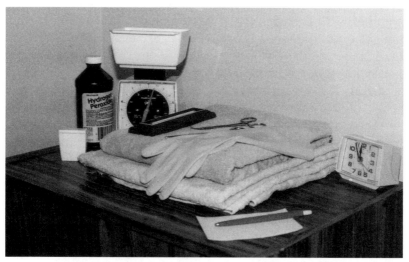

Some of the supplies required for a normal whelping.

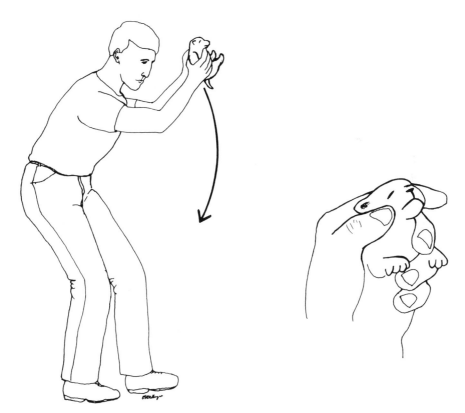

Shaking newborn puppies to resuscitate them.

jumping excessively high. If she landed on a puppy when returning, she might injure it. The adjustable sides are also useful for keeping active puppies from venturing outside of the box without consent.

Whelping boxes constructed with removable pig rails are also very useful. If the rails are left in the box too long, however, the puppies will use them to climb to freedom.

A heat lamp with a 250-watt infrared bulb may be set up to warm one corner of the whelping box when the bitch is absent from the box. Be certain that the puppies have plenty of room to crawl away from this source of heat. If the puppies cannot crawl away from the heat lamp, they may become overheated, dehydrate and die.

Delivery Supplies

Have a clock, a notepad and a pen in the whelping room to record the time that active labor begins and the time that each puppy is born. Use the baby scale to weigh each puppy and record each individual's weight. If necessary, mark each puppy so that you can identify them. Various methods are used to identify puppies. Some breeders clip hair from different quarters of each puppy of a given sex. Other breeders use food dyes to mark each puppy. Neither method is permanent. Most breeders use different colored ribbons as collars to identify individuals. If you use ribbons, be careful that no puppy gets a foot stuck in another puppy's collar.

A receiving box should be prepared in advance. A simple cardboard box lined with a heating pad set on the lowest setting and covered with a clean towel is all that is needed. Initially this box is used to store puppies while the bitch is in labor. Later it may be used to store puppies while the whelping box is being cleaned.

Sterile gloves are handy for use when you suspect that a puppy may be lodged in the pelvic birth canal.

Several supplies are needed to cut umbilical cords. A pair of hemostats, a pair of scissors, some dental floss and some hydrogen peroxide should be available.

A nursing kit should be prepared in case of a problem. It should include a brand-name puppy milk replacer, a pet baby bottle and a stomach tube. The powdered form of milk replacer is more economical than the canned form but requires mixing.

No whelping room would be complete without a rectal thermometer. The newer digital thermometers have a smaller diameter

This wooden whelping box is equipped with a solid floor. The ledge provides a convenient place to sit while observing or working with a litter and helps keep young puppies from wandering out of the box.

This wooden whelping box has no floor and sets up on a piece of indoor/outdoor carpeting. The projections on all four sides, called pig rails, can be removed as the puppies grow.

A variety of enclosures are routinely and successfully used by dog breeders as serviceable whelping quarters. Many bitches of large breeds, as has this Gordon Setter, have whelped and raised their litters in a child's wading pool.

and thus are easier and safer to use when taking the temperatures of neonates.

Normal Whelpings

Labor consists of three stages. During stage I, the bitch will act very anxious. She will be restless and will pace and nest. This stage may last from twelve to forty-eight hours and can be quite distressing for the novice breeder. Stage II is known as active labor and commences when the cervix is fully dilated. Strong uterine contractions occur and an abdominal press is obvious to onlookers. If sufficiently stressed by a noisy environment, bitches can voluntarily inhibit stage II. Stage III is the passing of each of the placentas, or afterbirths, and thus occurs concurrently with stage II.

If you have never assisted in the whelping of a litter before, you must secure a midwife in advance of the whelping. Certified veterinary technicians are often available. Find someone who has a great deal of experience whelping puppies and hire him or her if you must. Most midwives will deliver a litter for the price of one puppy. Since midwives save the lives of a great deal of puppies, the price they charge is very reasonable.

Try not to interfere with the bitch during stage I. When she starts nesting, calmly take her to her whelping box. Some bitches are comforted by the background noise of a radio or a television set playing in the whelping room. Be certain that the temperature of the room is between 85° and 90° F. If you live in an arid climate, place a humidifier in the room and set it between 55 and 60 percent. Do not allow strangers into the whelping room and limit the number of spectators to yourself.

Stage II labor may last from thirty minutes to three hours before the first puppy is born. If the bitch is actively contracting, stage II will last only thirty minutes. If she is contracting weakly, stage II may last for hours. Although the interval between puppies may vary, it should never exceed three hours.

Stage III, expulsion of the afterbirth, will usually follow the birth of each puppy. Occasionally, two puppies will be born and the two placentas will be passed simultaneously—just after the second puppy arrives. Be certain to count the number of placentas passed. There should be one placenta for each puppy. If the bitch retains a placenta, she may develop a severe uterine infection. Opinions vary on whether or not the bitch should be allowed to consume the placentas. There is no known medical reason to allow the consumption of placentas, and bitches that eat placentas tend to develop diarrhea.

The biggest flurry of activity will occur during stage II. A bubble representing a puppy in its sac will appear at the bitch's vulva. Occasionally the bubble will break, and the fluid released serves to lubricate the birth canal. Most often, however, the sac does not rupture. Allow nature to take its own course with the routine birth of a puppy in an unruptured sac, since the puppy has only a limited amount of time to begin breathing once the sac does rupture.

Sometimes it seems to take an inordinate amount of time for the entire puppy to be presented on the floor of the whelping box. Be patient. Never grab a puppy and begin tugging. Tugging on a puppy may inadvertently tear off a limb or rupture the umbilical stalk.

Usually the entire puppy will be born in its sac attached through the umbilical cord to the placenta. At this point the midwife should take the puppy away from the reaches of the bitch. I do not allow the bitch to consume the placenta. Some bitches are so nervous that they not only eat the placenta, they also begin consuming the umbilicus and may cause an umbilical hernia. When a puppy has a severe umbilical hernia, its intestines will protrude through the hernia. The puppy may often be saved if the bitch has not eaten any of its intestines. Take such a puppy away from the dam and call your veterinarian immediately.

Use a clean towel to rub the sac off the puppy. Begin with the puppy's head. Make certain to dry the nasal passages. Rub the puppy vigorously with the towel to stimulate respiration.

Many breeders and veterinarians use a technique known as shaking to stimulate newborns to breathe. To shake a puppy, you must grasp the puppy firmly in one hand with your index finger curved around the arch of the puppy's neck to provide a solid support for the neck. You must then cup your hands together and raise them above your head with the puppy's head pointed toward the ceiling. Your final action is to rapidly and forcefully drop your hands downward toward the floor. This removes fluid from the lungs of the puppy, and you will then need to wipe the puppy's nostrils with a clean towel.

Next the umbilical cord must be clamped, tied and severed. Take a hemostat and clamp it on the umbilical cord about one inch

This Maltese puppy was born with a severe umbilical hernia. Surgery was performed on the day he was born and he made a complete and successful recovery.

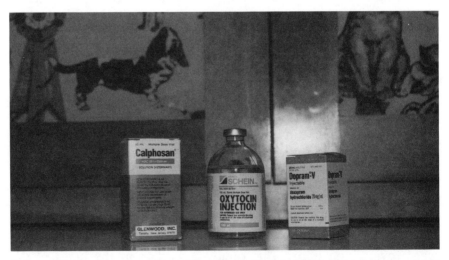

Drugs often used in connection with whelping include injectable calcium, oxytocin and doxapram, all manufactured under various brand names.

from the navel. Remove the hemostat and move it to approximately one and a half inches from the navel. With a pair of scissors, cut the placenta from the rest of the umbilicus and dispose of the placenta. Be certain to cut on the side of the hemostat away from the puppy's navel. The hemostat serves to crush the blood vessels and prevent them from bleeding. Take a piece of dental floss and tie it around the umbilicus at the spot where the hemostat was initially clamped—about one inch from the navel. Finally, remove the hemostat.

Healthy puppies will immediately appear vigorous. They will breathe with a strong, regular respiratory rate and will vocalize. Some weak puppies may be assisted by administering doxapram hydrochloride (Dopram). Dopram is a drug that stimulates respiration. Consult your veterinarian about this medication.

Healthy newborn puppies will also have a strong suckle reflex. That is, they will have a strong desire to nurse. After each puppy is delivered and has its umbilical cord cut, allow it to nurse until active contractions resume. Nursing serves two purposes at this time. First, nursing stimulates the release of oxytocin from the bitch's brain. Oxytocin, in turn, stimulates both milk letdown and uterine contractions. Second, nursing at this time provides the newborn puppy with colostrum. Colostrum is a special kind of milk only produced during the first twenty-four hours after whelping. It is special because it contains antibodies that the newborn can absorb and use to fend off infectious agents.

If you are uncertain as to whether or not the bitch has delivered all her puppies, call your veterinarian. He or she may recommend that you bring her to the hospital. At the hospital an X-ray can be taken to reveal any remaining puppies. Your veterinarian may also wish to give your bitch a shot of oxytocin. Many breeders refer to this as a "pit shot." The oxytocin will stimulate uterine contractions and therefore help to expel any retained placental material. Oxytocin is absolutely contraindicated if a bitch has an obstructed uterus, because the uterine contractions will cause the uterus to rupture if a puppy cannot be delivered naturally. Therefore, oxytocin should never to administered without direct veterinary supervision.

DYSTOCIA

Dystocia is the medical term for a difficult birth. It may be caused by a problem with either the dam or a puppy.

Maternal causes of dystocia include uterine and pelvic abnormalities. Uterine abnormalities include torsion, tears, herniations and inertia. Uterine torsion occurs when the uterus twists on itself. Once this occurs, no puppies can be born naturally. In some cases the uterus may actually tear during labor. A tear in the uterus will allow leakage into the abdominal cavity of the bitch and will cause her to become critically ill. Some bitches develop problems with inguinal hernias during pregnancy. The uterus will protrude through the inguinal ring and may become strangulated. Uterine inertia is the only common maternal cause of dystocia. Inertia may result from a number of primary causes. Hypocalcemia (low blood levels of calcium) and hypoglycemia (low blood levels of sugar) will cause inertia. Prolonged labor may also cause inertia if the muscle wall of the uterus becomes exhausted. Uterine torsion, tears and herniation must be treated surgically. Uterine inertia can sometimes be treated medically without surgical intervention.

Abnormalities of the bitch's pelvis may also cause dystocia. Some tiny bitches have a pelvic canal that is too small for average puppies to pass through. Many bitches that have been struck by automobiles suffer severe pelvic fractures. These pelvic fractures often heal in unusual anatomical positions. Bitches of the brachycephalic breeds—those that have flattened faces—tend to have very narrow pelvises. Dystocias caused by a pelvic abnormality must be treated surgically.

Problems with one or all of the puppies in a litter may cause dystocia. Puppies that die in utero do not stimulate the bitch's uterus to contract, which may lead to difficulties.

Any unusually large puppy may not be able to pass through the birth canal and may cause dystocia. Brachycephalic breeds tend to produce puppies with heads that are too large to pass through the dam's birth canal. Unusually large puppies are often seen in small or single-puppy litters. "Monster puppies" are sometimes conceived that have abnormally large heads or heads that are grossly enlarged by fluid retention.

A normal puppy may cause dystocia by being abnormally situated in the uterus. Contrary to popular opinion, breech positioning occurs in about half of all normal canine deliveries and does not cause a problem for delivery. However, a puppy in a transverse position will cause dystocia. A puppy presented in a transverse position presents neither its head nor its tail first. Rather, the side of the puppy is presented.

Puppies that are dead, abnormally sized or in a transverse position must be delivered by Caesarean section.

Dystocia should be considered and a veterinarian should be notified if any one of the following problems are encountered:

- If the length of gestation is markedly shortened or markedly lengthened. Normal gestation length will vary between fifty-eight and sixty-eight days. (Refer to the previous chapter for more detailed information on predicting a whelping date.)
- If the bitch has a vaginal discharge before the birth of the first puppy. A mucus discharge is normal; all other discharges are abnormal. A green discharge indicates that a placenta has detached from the uterus and that the associated puppy must be delivered soon or it will not survive. A bright red discharge indicates that the bitch is hemorrhaging. A puslike discharge indicates a uterine infection.
- If strong, active labor contractions last for more than thirty minutes.
- If the bitch is in obvious distress. Bitches in distress will hyperventilate and will have a weak, rapid pulse. A distressed bitch may vomit. Hypocalcemia may cause weakness, trembling or convulsions.
- If weak, nonproductive labor lasts for more than three hours before the first puppy is delivered.
- If more than three hours elapse between puppies. It is often difficult to determine whether or not all puppies have been delivered and, hence, when labor has actually ceased. If you have any doubt, consult your veterinarian. A shot of oxytocin may be indicated. An X-ray can be taken to make certain that all puppies have been safely delivered. The time interval between puppies is typically irregular.
- If fewer placentas than puppies are passed at the end of whelping.

Veterinarians make many different arrangements for emergency care of their clients. Some veterinarians handle all their own emergencies and are contacted after hours by an answering service. Other veterinarians, usually in metropolitan areas, refer their after-hours emergency calls to a centralized emergency facility. Be certain that you know in advance what arrangement your veterinarian has made for emergency care.

CAESAREAN SECTIONS

Much mystery surrounds the Caesarean section surgery. As indicated in the previous section on dystocia, a Caesarean, or "C-section," is often necessary to save the bitch and/or the puppies.

Most C-sections are done without an accompanying ovario-hysterectomy, or spay surgery. However, sometimes the bitch must be spayed in order to save her life. Such is the case with uterine rupture, for example. If the bitch is spayed, she may or may not be able to adequately nurse her litter. If the bitch need not be spayed, she may go on to have future litters even without a second C-section.

Anesthesia is the most difficult aspect of a C-section surgery. The goal is to adequately anesthetize the bitch with a drug that will not cross the placenta quickly enough to interefere with neonatal respiration.

Both a tranquilizer and an anticholinergic drug are commonly used as preanesthetic medications. The tranquilizer most often used is acepromazine maleate. It is used at very low doses to provide mild tranquilization, which helps to decrease the amount of general anesthesia needed for the C-section. It does, however, cause a decrease in blood pressure and may cross the placenta. An anticholinergic drug is given to offset the effects of the tranquilizer. Two anticholinergic drugs are available: atropine and glycopyrrolate (Robinul). Although atropine does cross the placenta, it does not have any known adverse effects on the fetuses.

General anesthesia is usually induced with an injectable, intravenous drug and then maintained by either an injectable or an inhalant anesthesia agent. Either a narcotic or a barbiturate may be used as injectable medications. Narcotics pass the placental barrier but can be reversed in either the bitch or the puppies if indicated with "antinarcotic" drugs. Barbiturate drugs cross the placenta rapidly, so their use may result in an increase in neonatal mortality.

Various inhalant anesthesia agents may be used to produce general anesthesia. In general, these gas machines are only suited to be used for a particular agent. Inhalant anesthesia may also cause depression in the neonate, but the effects are usually lost as the

116

newborn begins to breathe and expire the agent. In most cases, a local analgesic such as lidocaine is injected along the bitch's midline to minimize the amount of general anesthesia needed.

Most bitches recover from anesthesia rapidly and can be placed with their puppies to care for them shortly after awakening. Most bitches do not seem to mind having the puppies clamber over their incision postoperatively.

Timing is of the utmost importance when performing C-sections. If the surgery is performed too early in the pregnancy, the puppies will not be mature enough to survive. Alternately, if the surgery is performed too late, neither the bitch nor her puppies may survive. Therefore, records must be kept meticulously and pregnant bitches monitored closely.

Good nutrition is a critical component of postpartum care for a bitch and her litter. Nourishing food in ample quantities ensures a well-fed dam and, by extension, her growing puppies.

11

Postpartum Care
of the Dam

PUPPIES ARE DEFINED as neonates for the first three weeks of life and are very fragile during this period. The first seventy-two hours after birth are especially critical to survival of the bitch and her litter. If the bitch becomes ill, the puppies will also become ill. Therefore, the bitch's health must be monitored closely and any postpartum diseases must be readily recognized.

MONITORING THE DAM'S HEALTH

The bitch's rectal temperature should be taken daily for the first two weeks after whelping. It will be higher than it was before she delivered the litter, but it should never exceed 103° F. If the bitch becomes febrile, contact your veterinarian immediately.

While her temperature is being taken, the bitch's vulva should be examined and any vaginal discharge noted. Bitches normally have a discharge for three to four weeks after whelping. This normal discharge is called lochia and is usually thin to mucoid in consistency and reddish-brown in color. If the discharge noted is soupy in consistency or if it is yellow, bright red or greenish-black, it is probably abnormal and you should consult your veterinarian.

POSTPARTUM DISEASES

The health of the litter is in good measure contingent upon the health of the dam. A number of diseases commonly afflict bitches just after whelping. Some of them cause an obvious vaginal discharge. Postpartum diseases of the bitch that may cause a vaginal discharge include metritis, retained placentas, postpartum hemorrhage and subinvolution of placental sites. Other postpartum diseases of the bitch do not cause a vaginal discharge. They include hysteria, uterine prolapse, mastitis and eclampsia.

Any sick bitch that has just whelped a litter should be tested for brucellosis, as this disease may manifest itself in many ways.

Common postpartum diseases of the bitch will be discussed individually in detail.

Metritis

Metritis is an infection of the uterus. Signs of metritis include lethargy, lack of appetite, fever and an abnormal vaginal discharge. Often the puppies are also ill. The bitch will not be able to nurse her litter while she is ill. The only effective treatment in most cases is to spay the affected bitch. Occasionally an affected bitch may be treated effectively with antibiotics. Metritis may be caused by an underlying disease of the uterus preexistent to the pregnancy. Metritis may also be due to infection of the uterus incurred while whelping in association with instrument-assisted deliveries. The diagnosis of metritis may be supported by finding a high white blood cell count and an enlarged uterus with or without a retained fetus on an abdominal radiograph. The prognosis is good for the life of the dam but guarded for her future breeding potential.

Retained Placentas

A bitch should pass a placenta for each puppy born. If fewer placentas than puppies are passed, one or more placentas have been retained. This is an uncommon event and usually results from an abnormal parturition, or delivery. The presence of a copious, greenish-black discharge for more than two days after parturition is a sign that a placenta has been retained. Sometimes affected bitches are depressed and uninterested in food. They may or may not be febrile. The fetal membranes may break down on their own and pass without adverse effects on the bitch.

Bitches suspected of having a retained placenta should be observed closely. The rectal temperature of suspect bitches should be taken every eight hours. The vulva should be inspected for a puslike discharge every time the temperature is taken. Bitches with retained placentas may be treated with calcium and oxytocin to stimulate the uterus to expel the membranes within twenty-four hours of whelping. If more time elapses, the cervix will be closed and oxytocin may cause the uterus to rupture.

A retained placenta may lead to metritis. In such cases, surgery is the indicated method of treatment. The bitch may need to be spayed if the uterus has been irreversibly damaged.

Postpartum Hemorrhage

Postpartum hemorrhage is defined as unusually heavy bleeding after whelping. It is an uncommon event. The only obvious sign is an excessive amount of bloody vaginal discharge. Occasionally affected bitches may have pale gums secondary to a blood-loss anemia.

Postpartum hemorrhage has several causes. One cause is an inherent bleeding disorder, such as von Willebrand's disease. Injury to the vagina during instrument delivery is another cause of excessive bleeding. Occasionally hypocalcemia may cause hemorrhaging to occur. Postpartum hemorrhage may be diagnosed by examining a blood sample to detect the resultant blood-loss anemia. Appropriate treatment will depend upon the primary cause of the hemorrhage. Hypocalcemia is treated by administering calcium. Vaginal tears need to be sutured. If bleeding cannot be controlled, the bitch will need to be spayed. Transfusions will be necessary if the anemia is severe. Although the prognosis for future breeding potential of affected bitches varies, the prognosis is good for saving her life.

Subinvolution of Placental Sites

Subinvolution of placental sites (SIPS) is defined as incomplete healing of the wall of the uterus. Its cause is unknown. SIPS tends to occur primarily in first-litter bitches and usually occurs in bitches that are less than three years old. A low-grade, bloody vaginal discharge that persists for more than four weeks after whelping without any sign of metritis indicates that a bitch has SIPS.

In contrast to bitches afflicted with metritis, bitches with SIPS are bright, alert and responsive. Puppies remain healthy, and the uterus shrinks to a normal size. In contrast to many bitches with postpartum hemorrhage, bitches with SIPS have normal blood hemostasis. SIPS can only be definitively diagnosed by obtaining a sample of the wall of the uterus for biopsy, which necessitates surgery. Blood sampling can usually rule out metritis and postpartum hemorrhage. Bitches with metritis will have high white blood cell counts and bitches with postpartum hemorrhage will have low red blood cell counts.

Treatment of SIPS depends upon the severity of the disease and any resultant secondary problems. Antibiotics and transfusions are sometimes indicated. SIPS is such an uncommon occurrence that the prognosis is unknown for certain. Most often, the prognosis appears to be good.

Hysteria

Hysteria is defined as an abnormal display of maternal aggression. Affected bitches attack and/or kill their offspring. The savaged puppies are normal and healthy in all respects. The cause is unknown. Some breeders believe that hysteria is a bizarre display of hypocalcemia. Most afflicted bitches respond to a low dose of tranquilizer given in the morning. Sometimes, however, puppies must be removed from the dam and either fed by hand or raised by a foster mother. The prognosis is poor because hysteria may recur with the mother's next litter.

Uterine Prolapse

Uterine prolapse is a protrusion of all or part of a uterine horn to the exterior of the bitch's body. A prolapsed uterus can be seen extruding through the vulva. Uterine prolapse is rare and occurs immediately during or after parturition. It may or may not result from an instrument-assisted delivery of a puppy.

Treatment of uterine prolapse requires an exploratory surgery. If the uterus is not damaged, the bitch need not be spayed. If, however, the uterus has been irreparably damaged, the bitch will have to be spayed to save her life. The prognosis is good for the life of the bitch but poor for her future reproduction.

Mastitis

Mastitis is the infection of one or more mammary glands. It is usually caused by an ascending infection. In other words, bacteria on the surface of the skin covering the mammary gland enter the canal and travel upward toward the center of the gland. Signs of mastitis are obvious. Affected glands are enlarged, painful and warm to the touch. Most bitches are febrile. Occasionally a bitch may refuse to eat or to mother her young. A diagnosis of mastitis can be supported by an elevated white blood cell count. Milk from affected glands should be collected so that it may be cultured. Once the milk is cultured, the offending bacteria can be identified and appropriate antibiotics can be given to the bitch.

Warm soaks and a course of aspirin may alleviate the bitch's discomfort. Some infected glands are abscessed and thus must be lanced to drain for treatment to be effective. Young usually need not be weaned. If they do need to be weaned, the bitch's food intake should be decreased by half. If the glands become edematous during weaning, a diuretic may be given to alleviate the fluid retention.

Eclampsia

Eclampsia, or "milk fever," is a periparturient disease caused by low blood levels of calcium. In order to produce milk, calcium is preferentially taken from the bitch's bloodstream to be delivered to her mammary glands. Eclampsia may occur before, during or shortly after whelping. It usually occurs during heavy lactation—two to four weeks after whelping. Although any breed of dog may be affected, toy breeds are most often affected. In fact, toy bitches with large litters are at greatest risk.

Eclampsia is usually associated with poor nutrition. Signs vary depending upon the severity of the calcium deficiency. Most bitches are weak and have muscle tremors. Seizures may occur. Severe muscle tremors and seizures will cause the body temperature to rise markedly.

Eclampsia is diagnosed by testing a sample of blood to evaluate blood calcium levels. Bitches are treated by removing the puppies for twelve to twenty-four hours and administering calcium. The prognosis is poor because eclampsia often recurs during the same and subsequent lactations. If it recurs in the same lactation, the puppies will have to be weaned from the dam.

Table 11-1
Postpartum Diseases of the Bitch

Disease	Vaginal Discharge	Signs	Rx	Pups sick?	Prx—life	Prx—breeding
Metritis	+	Sick	Spay	+	Good	Poor
Retained placenta	+	±	Drugs or spay	±	Good	Var.
PPH	+	±	Var.	±	Good	Var.
SIPS	+	Well	Var.	−	Good	Good
Hysteria	−	Behavioral	Tranq.	±	Good	Poor
Uterine prolapse	−	Obvious	Surgery	−	Good	Poor
Mastitis	−	Obvious	Drugs	±	Good	Good
Eclampsia	−	Behavioral	Drugs	±	Var.	Poor

Rx–treatment
Prx–prognosis
Var.–variable
Tranq.–tranquilize

12

Care of Neonates

NEONATES WILL RECEIVE the best care from breeders who are well informed. Dog breeders should be aware of general principles regarding the management of newborns, and they should be able to recognize both congenital and acquired diseases. It is imperative that breeders understand the basic principles regarding the special treatment of neonates. It is also often helpful to know how to supplement and hand feed puppies.

GENERAL PRINCIPLES

All newborn puppies should receive colostrum within the first twenty-four hours after birth, unless the bitch is deceased. Colostrum is a special kind of milk made by the bitch for a short while after delivery. It contains antibodies that serve to protect newborns from common infectious diseases. These antibodies are very large molecules and can only be absorbed by the newborn for a short while after birth. They are essential to the future health of the puppy.

Some veterinarians recommend feeding newborns lactobacillus, a type of bacteria found in acidophilus milk, yogurt and some commercial products. This bacteria is often referred to as a "friendly" bacteria, necessary to help the puppy digest foods and to prevent "unfriendly" bacteria from establishing themselves within the digestive tract. Most people recommend that it be given on the second and fourth day of life. Lactobacillus causes no known ill effects when given to newborns.

It is essential to record the weight of all puppies. Twenty-four hours after birth, puppies will fall into one of three possible categories. The largest category of puppies is that in which the puppies gain weight. Another category of puppies loses less than 10 percent of their original body weight. These puppies are not in imminent danger but should be watched closely. The final category of puppies is that in which the puppies lose more than 10 percent of their body weight within the first twenty-four hours of life. These puppies must be watched very closely and should receive supplemental feedings.

Puppies should be weighed daily for the first week of life. Thereafter, once each week is adequate. Most puppies double their original birth weight by the time they are seven to ten days old. A good, general rule of thumb is that a newborn puppy should gain 10 percent of its birth weight daily.

Tails should be amputated and dewclaws should be removed between two and four days of age, as mandated by breed standards. Larger puppies should be done at two days of age, while smaller puppies should be done at four days of age. Most veterinarians will not do these procedures at birth because birth itself is a tremendous stress. Only two breed standards—the Briard and the Great Pyrenees—currently mandate that puppies should have and retain a double set of rear dewclaws. Many veterinary textbooks contain a chart to assist veterinarians in determining an appropriate tail length for each particular breed.

During the first three, critical weeks of a litter's life, the litter must be kept warm. Most experienced breeders will state adamantly, "A chilled pup is a dead pup!" Therefore, the whelping room should be maintained between 85° and 90° F for the first week. The temperature may be gradually decreased to 75° F by the end of the third week of life. Again, common sense should prevail. If the puppies are bright pink in color, remain separated from one another and are breathing with an open mouth, they are too hot. The room temperature must be decreased or the puppies will rapidly dehydrate and die.

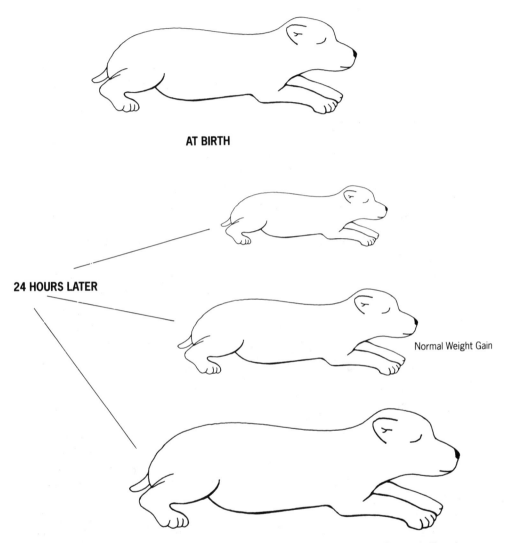

AT BIRTH

24 HOURS LATER

Normal Weight Gain

Newborn puppies will fall into one of three weight categories. Some will gain, some will lose less than 10 percent of their birth weight and some will lose more than 10 percent of their birth weight. Puppies that fall into the last category should be supplemented.

CONGENITAL DEFECTS

Shortly after birth, each puppy should be examined closely to identify any congenital defects. Please note that a congenital defect is an abnormality that is present at birth. It is not synonymous with a genetic defect. Some congenital defects are hereditary and thus caused by genetic defects. However, other congenital defects are not hereditary. They are caused by environmental influences, such as exposure of the pregnant bitch to drugs.

Certain deformities are relatively commonplace and should be ruled out with a physical examination of each newborn puppy. Each puppy's chest, spine, limbs and tail should be evaluated and deemed normal. *Pectorus excavatum* is the medical term for flat chest, and it may be the cause of future swimmer puppies. Newborns sometimes sustain rib fractures during birth. As the affected puppy grows, its ability to breathe may be impaired. Tail deformities such as kinks in the tail are common in certain breeds, such as the Irish Setter. The spine should be straight when viewed from above. If it is not, the puppy may have lordosis or kyphosis, congenital curvatures of the spine. Any one of the limbs may be shortened secondary to a tendon contracture or an absent bone. Joint swellings, if any, should be examined by a veterinarian; they may be infected. If so, without appropriate medical care the joint will be rapidly destroyed. Occasionally puppies are born with an abnormal number of toes. In general, if the puppy has the two center toes and the central pad, it will be able to ambulate adequately as an adult.

Newborn puppies should be evaluated for normal mobility. Normal puppies will have a rooting reflex and a suckling reflex at birth that enables them to find the mother's supply of milk. Normal puppies should also be able to move all four limbs and their tails.

Two common congenital defects are cleft palate and anal atresia. Cleft palates are easily identified by examining the roof of the mouth. Affected puppies will have a split in the center of the roof. Anal atresia is a condition in which the anus fails to open. As a result, affected puppies cannot defecate. Puppies with either a cleft palate or anal atresia are usually euthanized at birth.

While the newborn's head is being examined for a cleft palate, it should also be evaluated to identify an open fontanelle. An open fontanelle on a puppy with a dome-shaped head often indicates that a puppy has hydrocephalus. This is a common congenital defect in certain breeds, such as the Chihuahua. The eyelids of a newborn

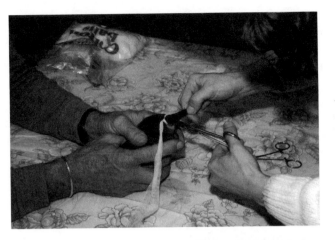

Tails are normally docked when puppies are between two and four days old.

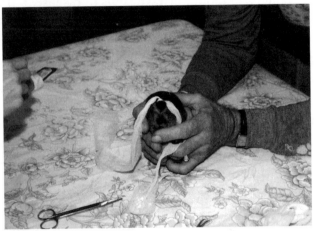

After docking is completed, it is wise to keep the puppies apart from their dam long enough to make sure she will not initiate fresh bleeding.

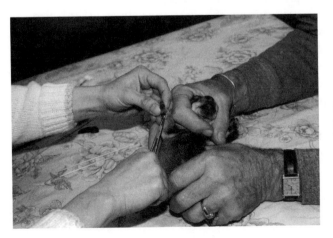

Dewclaws should be removed at the same time tails are docked.

should also be examined closely, as an infection under the closed eyelids may lead to permanent damage to the affected puppy's eyes. Any nasal discharge should be noted and reported to a veterinarian immediately.

SIGNS OF NEONATAL ILLNESS

It is difficult to evaluate the overall health status of newborns. This is primarily due to the fact that the bitch takes care of all the puppies' needs. We cannot objectively evaluate how much a newborn puppy is eating, whether or not the puppy is depressed or even if it has diarrhea. We can, however, alert ourselves to watch for some common, outward signs of disease in newborn puppies. These signs include abdominal distention, swollen eyelids, bleeding, crusted skin, poor mobility, improper weight gain, low body temperature and excessive activity. As neonates age, we can often begin looking for other signs of disease, such as vomiting, diarrhea and regurgitation. Each of these signs will be discussed individually.

Abdominal Bloating

Swelling of a neonate's abdomen may indicate one of three possible neonatal illnesses: navel ill, toxic milk syndrome and ascariasis.

Navel ill results from an infection of the umbilicus, often caused by bacteria within the bitch's mouth at the time that she severed the umbilical cord. Most affected puppies have a blue tinge to their abdomens. It usually occurs within the first four days of life and must be treated aggressively with antibiotic therapy. Navel ill occurs sporadically; most often, only one or two puppies are affected.

Toxic milk syndrome results from a systemic maternal infection. The systemic maternal infection is usually caused by metritis or subinvolution of placental sites and is passed to the puppies through the milk. This syndrome may occur anytime during the first two weeks of life and usually affects all puppies in the litter. Puppies must be temporarily removed from their dam while her systemic infection is being treated.

Ascariasis is caused by an overwhelming roundworm burden. Affected puppies should be dewormed and maintained on a premium food if they are eating solid food. While being treated, puppies should be monitored closely, as the dead worms may impact a puppy's intestines.

Swelling of the Eyelids

Puppies that develop conjunctivitis before their eyes open may incur irreparable damage to their eyes if not treated promptly and aggressively. Treatment entails opening any eyelids still sealed and dosing with antibiotics. It is important to carefully open the eyelids of all the puppies in a litter, because multiple puppies are usually affected with the conjunctivitis.

Bleeding

A hemorrhagic syndrome is occasionally seen in puppies less than four days old. Signs of the syndrome include bloody urine and bleeding from the nostrils. The syndrome is believed to be due to a deficiency of vitamin K in affected puppies, since this vitamin is essential to normal blood clotting. Therefore, affected puppies are treated with vitamin K. On occasion it is also necessary to treat affected puppies with a fresh plasma transfusion, since plasma contains clotting factors.

Crusted Skin Lesions

Isolated areas of crusty, hairless skin may be found on the head and neck of puppies with staphylococcal infections. Infected puppies are typically four to ten days old. The staph infection probably occurs when the dam neglects to clean this area of the puppy. Antibacterial cleansing agents and oral antibiotics are used to treat infected puppies.

Improper Locomotion

Flat puppies, also referred to as "swimmer puppies," are readily identified because they do not ambulate normally. They appear flat from chest to backbone and appear to swim rather than walk. Most puppies begin to stand after their eyes open and should walk on shaky legs by three weeks of age. Management practices predispose some toward becoming swimmer puppies. Therefore, every effort should be made to provide neonatal puppies with secure footing. Certain short-faced breeds of puppies are predisposed. This predisposition is probably related to conformation. Affected puppies are sometimes aided by hobbling their back legs together with tape.

Lack of Weight Gain

National breed clubs would be well advised to collect data on normal birth weights for their individual breeds, as there is a paucity of information on normal birth weights relative to each breed. Suffice it to say that puppies significantly smaller than the breed average have a much higher mortality.

Each individual's weight should be recorded at birth and at daily intervals for the first week of life. As previously discussed, newborns will fall into one of three weight-gain categories. Puppies that lose more than 10 percent of their birth weight within the first twenty-four hours of life are in a critical condition and should be supplemented. In general, newborns should double their birth weight by the time they are seven to ten days old. As another general rule, newborns should gain 10 percent of their original birth weight each day until weaning.

Hypothermia

Most bitches will cull cold puppies. Keep in mind that a bitch may cull a puppy for many other reasons, such as congenital malformations.

Excessive Activity

Normal puppies spend 90 percent of the time sleeping. They have occasional muscle twitching or activated sleep until they are about four weeks old. Sick puppies often vocalize excessively. They may cry continuously for fifteen minutes or more. Excessive crying is usually the first sign noted by breeders in puppies infected with herpes virus. Herpes is an acute, viral disease that affects puppies one to three weeks of age. Although all puppies in a litter are usually infected, not all puppies show signs at the same time. Most crying puppies infected with herpes die within twenty-four hours. Since the herpes virus cannot survive at adult dog body temperatures, treatment includes elevating the environmental temperature. Puppies already showing signs may be saved, only to go on and develop

132

kidney failure at a very young age. Necropsy will provide a definitive diagnosis of herpes, since an infected puppy will have severe bleeding in its kidneys and liver. Subsequent litters borne by the bitch will be unaffected.

Vomiting Solid Food

When weaning is begun at about three weeks of age, puppies should be monitored closely for any signs of impending illness. Diarrhea is not uncommon as a result of the dietary change. Vomiting, however, is unusual and indicates a potentially serious problem.

Intestinal impaction with roundworms is a common cause of vomiting seen in young puppies. Again, look for a distended abdomen and have a fecal sample examined for parasite eggs.

Pyloric stenosis is a congenital disease of the stomach. It is caused by a narrowing of the outlet from the stomach and results in projectile vomiting. The projectile vomiting, however, is not noted until solid food is introduced.

Diarrhea

Diarrhea is often impossible to detect in neonatal puppies because the mother usually stimulates elimination and keeps the whelping box free of debris. Occasionally, a puppy's stool will be observed by the breeder. Normal neonatal stool is yellow-brown in color, slightly formed in consistency. It includes curdles of partially digested milk. Green stool is not normal and is usually due to rapid passage through the puppy's digestive system. Yellow stool indicates that the feces are too acidic; if this is the case, one to three milliliters of milk of magnesia should be administered twice daily for one or two days. White stool indicates a lack of digestion and is a serious sign. Whenever white stools are detected, a veterinarian should be contacted. If diarrhea truly exists in the neonate, one to three milliliters of Pepto-Bismol may be administered two to three times daily. Any neonate with diarrhea should have a stool sample examined for intestinal parasites.

Regurgitation

It is important to distinguish between vomiting and regurgitation. Vomiting is an active event. The stomach contents are expelled from the mouth of a vomiting dog by heaving motions. Regurgitation is a passive event that occurs rapidly without any retching. It usually occurs shortly after eating. Regurgitated food is cylindrical in form.

Three relatively common congenital defects will cause puppies to regurgitate solid foods: cleft palate, idiopathic megaesophagus and persistent right aortic arch (PRAA).

Cleft palate will cause puppies to regurgitate milk. It has been noted in almost all breeds. Affected puppies are usually euthanized.

Idiopathic megaesophagus is most often seen in German Shepherd Dogs. It is caused by a weak, dilated esophaghus. The esophagus is the tube that transports food from the mouth to the stomach. Megaesophagus is treated by feeding affected dogs from an elevated height.

PRAA is often seen in Irish Setters. It is caused by a defect in the blood vessels associated with the heart. The offending blood vessel surrounds the esophagus and strangulates it. Puppies affected with PRAA may sometimes be treated surgically. They, too, may be fed from elevated heights.

TREATING SICK NEONATES

Sick neonates must be kept warm. They have no shivering reflex for the first week of life and do not tend to develop fevers as do sick adult dogs. Instead, sick neonates tend to become hypothermic.

Hypothermia is defined as a body temperature below normal. Normal neonatal body temperature is not the same as normal adult body temperature. Normal neonatal temperature ranges between 94° and 97° F for the first two weeks of life. Between two and four weeks of age, the body temperature normally ranges between 97° and 99° F. After four weeks of age, the puppy's body temperature should approach that of an adult, 101° to 102° F.

Once the body temperature drops, the digestive system ceases working. Therefore, food should be withheld from a sick neonate until its body temperature is gradually raised to normal.

Sick neonates usually are ineffective nursers and, hence, become dehydrated. Rehydration with subcutaneous and oral fluids is essential to successful treatment of the ill neonate. Once the puppy is warmed and rehydrated, feeding should resume so that hypoglycemia does not ensue. If the neonate is removed from its dam, it should be stimulated to urinate and defecate.

Any puppy that dies should be taken to a veterinarian so that a necropsy may be performed. A necropsy will often indicate whether other puppies in the litter are in danger of becoming ill.

SUPPLEMENTING LARGE LITTERS

When a bitch has a large litter, some or all of her puppies may need supplemental feedings. There are two basic schemes to choose from when faced with the need to supplement. Some of the puppies may be taken from the mother and fed entirely by hand, or all the puppies may be left with the mother and all may be fed by hand in between maternal feedings.

If some of the puppies are taken from the mother, they should be identified as "tail enders." Tail enders are those puppies that have never had a strong grip on life. They are often from the group of puppies that lost more than 10 percent of their body weight within the first twenty-four hours of life. They should not be fed for two to four hours after being taken from the mother to ensure that her milk and the milk replacer do not mix within the puppy's stomach. They may be given water during this time, however.

If the entire litter is to be supplemented, they should be supplemented halfway between maternal feedings. There are many advantages to leaving the puppies with their mother. She keeps them warm, clean and disciplined.

If supplemental feeding is necessary, the bitch should be examined by a veterinarian to ensure that no illness is preventing her from producing enough milk. Her nutritional status should also be closely scrutinized and improved if necessary.

HAND FEEDING PUPPIES

Hand feeding may become necessary if the mother dies, develops hysteria or cannot nurse the entire litter alone.

When puppies are hand fed, their environment must be kept warm and clean. During the first two weeks of life, the puppies should be separated from one another. This will prevent them from harming one another by nursing on each other. This also means that the environmental temperature must be closely monitored. Warmth is especially important for the neonate because the newborn puppy has no shivering reflex and very small stores of energy. After two weeks of age, the eyes and ears will open and puppies should be allowed to socialize with one another. During the first two weeks of life, the puppies should also receive anogenital stimulation to allow for adequate urination and defecation. Moistened cotton swabs should be rubbed over the anus and the genitals after each feeding.

When a newborn is not eating, it should be sleeping. Hence, newborns should be placed on a strict feeding schedule. Three daily feedings are usually adequate. Feed more often only if the puppies are crying and otherwise acting hungry.

Puppies should be fed a commercial bitch milk replacer. Neither goat nor cow milk is adequate. Only enough milk replacer for a single day's use should be mixed in advance. Between feedings, the milk replacer should be refrigerated. Just prior to feeding, the milk replacer should be warmed to room temperature or greater.

Three general rules apply to hand feeding puppies. First, any changes in feed must be made gradually. Second, the puppies must not be overfed or they will develop diarrhea. If the stools become loose and green, the volume of food should be decreased. Finally, chilled puppies should not be fed. Hypothermia will cause the digestive system to cease working and food will do more harm than good. Chilled puppies must be warmed and hydrated before feeding can resume.

Puppies may be either hand fed with a bottle or tube fed. Bottle feeding is time consuming but safe. Tube feeding is rapid but hazardous for the novice. The two hazards to avoid when tube feeding are aspiration and excessive distention. If a puppy is improperly tube fed, milk will be delivered to the lungs instead of the stomach and will cause an aspiration pneumonia. Overfeeding a puppy will cause excessive distention. Bottle-fed puppies will reject the bottle when they are full and are therefore not as likely as tube-fed orphans to aspirate or overfeed.

If you must tube feed puppies, secure a number 8, twelve-inch human infant rubber feeding tube, a 30-milliliter syringe and expert assistance. The first step is to determine how much of the tube to insert into the puppy. This is done by placing the tail end of the tube beside the puppy's last rib. The tube is then extended until the other end reaches the puppy's nostrils. The tube should be marked

Newborns must be stimulated to urinate and defecate for the first few weeks of life.

Healthy neonates have a plump appearance and sleep most of the time. Watch for involuntary twitching in sleeping puppies. This is called activated, or hyperkinetic, sleep and is a reliable sign of good health.

Improved knowledge of neonatal nutritive requirements and modes of feeding have made supplementing far more effective than it was even fairly recently. Bitches' milk substitutes approach natural formulations closely, and the use of nursing bottles, eye droppers or tubes makes getting food into puppies extremely efficient.

137

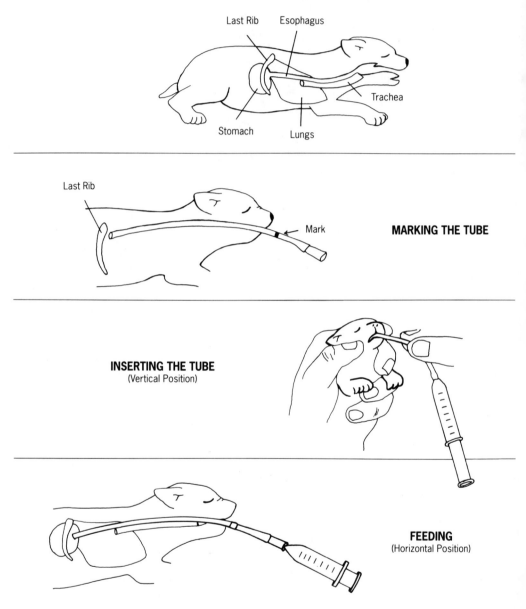

ANATOMY

Last Rib   Esophagus

Trachea

Stomach   Lungs

MARKING THE TUBE

Last Rib

Mark

INSERTING THE TUBE
(Vertical Position)

FEEDING
(Horizontal Position)

Tube feeding puppies as described in the text.

at a point three-quarters of the distance from the puppy's nostrils to its last rib. Because the puppy will grow rapidly, the marking should be checked weekly.

The next step is to place the tube into the puppy's mouth while holding the puppy in an upright position. Young puppies have no gag reflex and will, therefore, not gag when the tube is in the right location. However, they will often cough if the tube is inappropriately placed in the windpipe. To ensure that the tube is not in the windpipe, .5 milliliter of sterile water should be injected before actually feeding the puppy. If the puppy coughs with the water, remove the tube and insert it properly.

Finally, the puppy is placed in a horizontal position for the actual feeding. The syringe should be filled with warm milk replacer and all air should be ejected from the syringe. This will prevent the puppy from ingesting excessive amounts of air. The syringe is then attached to the rubber tube and food is injected slowly. Only 2 milliliters should be injected at one time. The puppy should be allowed thirty to sixty seconds between injections. If the puppy is fed too fast, it will aspirate. If the plunger of the syringe is forced with great pressure, the puppy will be overfed.

Whether tube feeding or bottle feeding, it is often difficult to determine how much to feed. When determining how much to feed, a few conversions must be learned and committed to memory. One ounce equals 30 milliliters. One tablespoon equals 15 milliliters. And 1 teaspoon equals 5 milliliters. In other words, each ounce contains 2 tablespoons or 6 teaspoons. Each tablespoon contains 3 teaspoons.

The stomach capacity of a puppy up to one week old is about 25 milliliters per pound of body weight. In other words, an eight-ounce puppy will be able to hold a maximum of 12.5 milliliters of food in its stomach. This is slightly less than a tablespoon. A puppy weighing twenty-four ounces will be able to maximally hold about 37.5 milliliters. This is slightly more than an ounce plus a teaspoon.

To hand feed a puppy, first calculate its stomach capacity. Offer it this much milk replacer by bottle at each of the three daily feedings for two days. Orphans will reject the bottle when full. If the orphan rejects the bottle, decrease the volume offered accordingly. If the orphan develops diarrhea, it is being overfed. Either decrease the volume fed or dilute the milk replacer. It is not unusual to have a small decrease in body weight for the first few days after hand feeding commences.

Tube feeding may only commence after two days of bottle feedings, provided that there has been no diarrhea or weight loss. For both tube- and bottle-fed puppies, increase the volume fed by one milliliter per feeding. Again, tube-fed puppies cannot reject the bottle and, therefore, must be fed slowly and with caution. The plunger of the syringe should never be forced.

Hand feed only as long as is absolutely necessary. Most puppies will begin to lap milk from a saucer when their eyes open at two to three weeks of age. Solid food should be introduced gradually, beginning at three weeks of age. Initially, a canned puppy food may be blended with the milk replacer. Dry puppy food may be added gradually to the mixture and the milk replacer may be eliminated. By five weeks of age, most puppies can eat solid food.

Table 12-1
Signs of Neonatal Illness

Sign	Age (days)	All pups?	Treatment
Navel ill	0–4	No	Antibiotics
Toxic milk	0–14	Yes	Remove pups and treat bitch
Ascariasis	Any	Yes	Deworm
Conjunctivitis	0–14	Yes	Open and treat eyes
Bleeding	0–4	No	Vitamin K
Skin staph	4–10	No	Antibiotics and cleansing
Swimmers	14–21	No	Change bedding, hobble
Fading	0–21	No	Supplement
Hypothermia	0–14	No	Warm slowly
Herpes	7–21	Yes	Warm slowly
Vomiting	21+	±	Variable
Diarrhea	21+	±	Variable
Regurgitation	21+	±	Surgery

13

Responsible Puppy Sales

VETERINARIANS RECOMMEND private breeders for several reasons. One is that privately bred puppies are often in better health than are other puppies. Another reason is that private breeders often educate novice puppy buyers. Concerned breeders will carefully select puppy buyers and will discuss potential behavioral and physical problems with each new buyer. The novice puppy owner needs to learn about many basics, such as housetraining and routine preventive care; a breeder can teach the novice these. Conversations between a breeder and a buyer can be minimized by providing each buyer with a wealth of literature and a good bibliography.

By educating buyers, breeders can keep their puppies healthy—both mentally and physically. Most breeders have had puppies returned or, worse yet, had to reclaim a puppy or two. In fact, some puppies behave like Australian boomerangs. Puppies that have been returned that are mentally and physically sound are much more pleasantly received. Therefore, even breeders who lack altruistic urges can benefit by spending time with buyers before sales are completed.

This chapter will discuss how to select puppy buyers, how to match each buyer with an appropriate puppy, how to evaluate a puppy's temperament and how to send useful information home with new owners.

INTERVIEWING POTENTIAL PUPPY BUYERS

Puppy buyers should be chosen very carefully in order to minimize the number of boomerangs encountered. Several questions should be posed to any potential buyer.

The most important question is "What happened to your last dog?" If the prospective buyer begins by saying that his eight-month-old Beagle ran out of the kitchen door and was struck by a car, the conversation should be terminated. If, on the other hand, the person says that his twelve-year-old Setter died sleeping behind the sofa, the breeder should keep listening. Some interested parties have never owned a dog before. These people should be questioned about their general life-style to determine whether or not a dog will comfortably fit into their lives.

Another important question is "Where will the puppy live?" A kennel run is one thing; a box with a chain is another. If the puppy will live in the house, the puppy should have a secure, fenced yard. A picture is always worth a thousand words. Thus, it is always interesting to request that prospective buyers bring pictures of their previous pets and of their current homes to the interview. The typical puppy buyer goes home believing that the typical dog breeder is crazy anyway.

Finally, a potential puppy buyer should be asked why he or she chose this breed. Potential buyers may have some serious misconceptions regarding a given breed of dog. Many families spend hours of time researching breeds in their local libraries. Unfortunately, better sources of information are not readily available to these families. If a buyer has a serious misconception regarding a breed, he or she will eventually regret the sale—and the puppy will ultimately suffer the most harm.

MATCHING PUPPIES AND BUYERS

After a buyer is found to be acceptable, he or she should be matched to an appropriate puppy. It can be difficult to fit a prospective owner with a suitable puppy. People and dogs are all individuals with unique personalities.

The buyer should be questioned to determine what personality characteristics he or she considers desirable. Does the buyer want a male or a female dog? Does the buyer prefer an active or a sedate animal? Does the buyer enjoy the company of an affectionate or an independent pet? These and other questions can be used to determine what the buyer prefers.

Some buyers want a dog that would not be a good match for them. If a sixty-year-old widow requests an active, independent male Mastiff, she should be refused because such a dog would be a poor choice for her. Prospective puppy buyers can either listen to reason or look elsewhere for a puppy.

Each litter should be both subjectively and objectively evaluated in order to ascertain individual temperament traits. Simple observation will quickly pinpoint some personality traits for each puppy. One way to evaluate each puppy's personality objectively is to have the litter aptitude tested by a qualified tester at the breeder's home or kennel.

PUPPY APTITUDE TESTING

Unfortunately, many breeders are not yet familiar with the notion of puppy aptitude testing. The puppy aptitude test (PAT) was designed to predict adult temperament. It evaluates several components of temperament, such as interest in socializing with people, degree of dominance, curiosity and sensitivity to both sight and sound. (See Table 13-1 on pp. 150–54.)

The person conducting the test should be very experienced in order to perform and interpret the results accurately. This will minimize human error. The tester should also be a stranger to the puppies being evaluated. This will maximize objectivity. Puppies should be tested at seven weeks of age in an unfamiliar area. A room in your home *reserved* for this purpose is suggested. This will prevent the puppies from being influenced by environmental factors.

The PAT is strongly recommended for identifying the right puppy for the right new family. It is not only a lot of fun but is also extremely useful in comparing puppies within a litter.

Wendy Volhard pioneered the PAT concept, and it has strongly impacted dog-raising practices today.

The method is briefly described in the sample score sheet. It is very important that the method employed be performed consistently. Otherwise, puppies cannot be compared with one another. The methods used are standardized and can be demonstrated by an experienced tester.

The social attraction and following subtests were designed to evaluate a puppy's attachment to people. The restraint and elevation dominance subtests were designed to evaluate a puppy's desire to dominate. Social dominance reveals a puppy's ability to bounce back following a disagreeable experience, and the retrieving subtest was designed to evaluate a puppy's willingness to work with people. The touch sensitivity subtest was designed to evaluate what training techniques would succeed with a specific puppy. The sound sensitivity subtest was designed to evaluate a puppy's reaction to loud noises; sound sensitivity can trigger a flight reaction in such cases. Finally, the sight sensitivity subtest was designed to evaluate a puppy's degree of curiosity and chase instinct.

The sample score sheet lists possible responses for each subtest. The score that a puppy will obtain for any given subtest depends upon its particular response. Scores for each subtest range from 1 to 6. Each subtest is scored independently of the other subtests, and subtest scores are never tallied.

Several generalizations can be made regarding the scores. A score of 1 is rare and indicates that the puppy will be aggressive. A very bold puppy will score a 2. A score of 3 indicates that the puppy is self-confident. A submissive puppy will score 4. A score of 5 indicates that the puppy is shy. An independent puppy (not interested in dogs or people) will score a 6.

Look for an overall pattern when interpreting test results. A puppy that scores 1s is not suitable for training, showing or breeding; it will be aggressive. A puppy scoring 2s will probably be domineering and will need a knowledgeable owner. Show prospects should score mostly 1s, 2s and 3s. Puppies that score mostly 4s usually make adoring pets. Quiet homes should be sought for those puppies that score many 4s and 5s.

If there is a large discrepancy between the test results and the breeder's intuition, the test should be repeated the next day. This will help to ensure that no puppy is tested on an off day.

For a more detailed discussion on test interpretation, please refer to the article entitled "Puppy Personality Profile," written by Gail Tamases and Wendy Volhard and appearing in the March 1985 issue of *Pure-Bred Dogs—American Kennel Gazette*. This article gives some excellent recommendations on matching individual puppies with individual buyers. It also makes some suggestions on picking outgoing show prospects. Again, the PAT should be explored with someone who has experience with the test. And the PAT should be expected to provide a lot of fun!

PUPPY CARE KITS

Each puppy should be sent to its new home with a puppy care kit, which may include a copy of its PAT results. Puppy care kits impart an image of professionalism that impresses owners. Many dog food companies will provide these kits free of charge, simply for the asking. Puppy care kits usually include the following:

- Sample of dog food and coupons
- Health record
- Container for a stool sample
- PAT results
- Guidelines for housetraining
- Sales contract
- AKC blue slip and pedigree
- Applications to breed clubs
- Book list for new puppy buyers
- Educational pamphlets on common ailments

The Crate as a Housetraining Aid

It is important to know that most pet owners have a difficult time housetraining puppies. Most pet owners are ignorant of the advantages of crate training and adamantly believe that crates are inhumane in spite of their parallel to a dog's natural den. As a result, many people live with dogs that have never truly been housetrained. Unfortunately, some of these people deposit their dogs at local humane societies because they cannot solve the problem.

Breeders can help to prevent many elimination behavior problems by discussing the advantages of crate training with new buyers. A puppy training crate can be included with each sale by adding a nominal fee to the basic price of each puppy.

Puppies learn to sleep comfortably in crates, and puppy buyers should get a clear explanation of why crates are so beneficial for their new puppies.

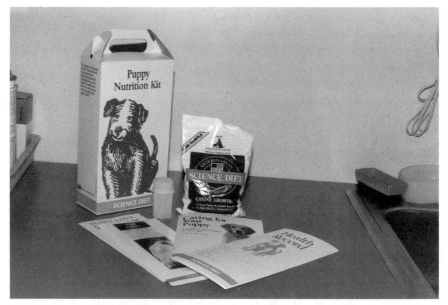

Many of the major dog food manufacturers make and distribute puppy-care kits for breeders to send with puppies going to new homes.

Contracts

Different breeders have different opinions regarding contracts. Some breeders expect buyers to sign on the dotted line with their own blood. Other breeders will never use a written contract. When contracts are written, they may be designed to protect the breed and to educate puppy buyers.

The breed can be protected by writing a clause into the contract that requires the buyer to screen for one or more genetic diseases. If a genetic disease is uncovered, the contract may stipulate that the puppy be neutered to protect both the breed and the breeder. Regardless of the results of such screening tests, information gathered from all puppies sold will help the breeder to make decisions wisely regarding future breedings.

The sample contract included below was written for the sale of English Setters and contains a clause that requires buyers to screen for hip dysplasia. Other contracts can be designed with specific breed predispositions in mind. Another clause in the sample contract is devoted to normal care of the puppy. The contract includes this clause because the general public is often ignorant of vaccination protocols and methods of parasite control. The buyer will have the opportunity, while reading this clause, to ask the breeder to clarify anything he or she does not understand.

Although kindergarten puppy classes taught at large obedience clubs can be fraught with problems, they can also be useful in assuring that each puppy is at least socialized. Boomerangs that have been socialized have many opportunities for a bright future. If the puppy actually learns some basic obedience at the class, it will be less likely to go on and develop behavior problems at home.

A contract is also a good way to introduce the novice to national and local breed clubs.

Sample Contract: Contract for Sale of an English Setter Puppy

COLOR:_____SEX:_____LITTER REG. NO.:_____DOB:_____
SIRE:_____DAM:_____
MARKINGS:_____
SOLD AS:_____PURCHASE PRICE:_____

In purchasing the puppy described above, I agree to the following as indicated by my initials by each requirement and my signature below:

_____1.　If at any time this puppy is to be sold or given away, the breeder is to be notified in writing by certified mail and given first option to buy the puppy back at or below the original purchase price.

_____2.　Buyer agrees to have this puppy's pelvis radiographically evaluated between August 2, 1992, and February 2, 1993, and submitted to the OFA for evaluation. The breeder must be notified in writing of the results. Buyer agrees by initialing this section that, should this requirement not be met, the breeder has the right to have radiographs taken by the veterinarian of her choice at the buyer's expense.

_____3.　Buyer agrees to exercise normal care in maintaining this puppy's health. Routine preventive care includes the following: annual physical examinations by a licensed veterinarian, annual vaccinations against DHLPP, annual fecal examinations, annual screening tests for heartworm detection and rabies vaccinations as mandated by the buyer's state of residence. Heartworm preventive is strongly recommended. Kennel cough vaccinations are also recommended, especially before boarding or showing. Normal care also assumes that the buyer maintain a fenced yard with access to the house. Normal care also assumes that the buyer will feed only nationally recognized brands of dog food.

_____4.　Buyer agrees to register the puppy for a puppy kindergarten class and to take the puppy to a majority of the classes before the puppy is six months old.

_____5.　Buyer agrees to register the puppy with the AKC by February 2, 1991, and to notify the breeder of the puppy's registered name. The registered name must include the prefix "Kaliber's."

_____6.　Buyer agrees to apply for membership to the English Setter Association of America by February 2, 1991.

_____7.　Buyer agrees to maintain the futurity status of the puppy with the ESSA. The first enrollment is due November 2, 1990. The second enrollment is due by February 2, 1991. June 1, 1991, is the deadline for the final enrollment. The buyer must be a member of the ESAA at the time of the final enrollment.

_____　　　_____
Signature of Buyer & Date　　　　　　　Signature of Breeder & Date

148

Bibliography

Puppy buyers are frequently anxious to read about their new charges. Breeders can help them by providing a bibliography of recommended books.

An additional fee may be added to the basic price of a puppy to include one exceptional book on puppy care or a book devoted to the breed. If a novice is buying a show prospect, he or she should at least be willing to read about the breed or about showing dogs. If the buyer has the books already, he or she isn't a novice; if the buyer doesn't have the books, he or she should be more than willing to purchase them. Most books cost about the same as an entry fee. If a buyer cannot purchase one book, how many shows can he afford to enter?

There is no need for breeders to feel mercenary when selling crates, books, toys or even dog food. Most pet stores send new puppy buyers off with an outrageous supply of overpriced items.

Informative Pamphlets

Many pamphlets are free for the asking from drug manufacturers. They can be distributed to new puppy buyers in order to teach them about heartworm, kennel cough and other preventable diseases.

Literature is also available from many veterinarians. Subjects of interest to new owners might include hip dysplasia, progressive retinal atrophy, hypothyroidism and epilepsy.

HOUSE-TRAINING

If you consistently follow a few simple rules, your new puppy can be *reliably* house-trained within a few weeks. Remember, the key word when training a dog is *consistency*.

Don't Permit Your Puppy to Urinate or Defecate Anywhere in the House.

Avoid "paper training" if possible since you will eventually have to try to teach your puppy to go outside anyway.

Table 13-1 Puppy Aptitude Test
The New Concise Chart and Scoresheet

Test and Purpose	Score	Comments
Social Attraction		
Purpose: Degree of attraction to people.	Comes readily, tail up, jumps, bites at hands...................1	
Method: Place pup in testing area 4 feet from tester, who coaxes puppy to her/him.	Comes readily, tail up, paws, licks at hands....................2	
	Comes readily, tail up 3	
	Comes readily, tail down 4	
	Comes hesitantly, tail down 5	
	Does not come at all 6	
Following		
Purpose: Degree of willingness to follow human leadership.	Follows readily, tail up, gets underfoot, bites at feet............1	
Method: Stand up and walk away from puppy, encouraging verbally.	Follows readily, tail up, gets underfoot 2	
	Follows readily, tail up............3	
	Follows readily, tail down 4	
	Follows hesitantly, tail down........5	
	Does not follow or goes away........6	

150

Restraint

Purpose: Degree of dominance or submission. Response to social/physical dominance.

Method: Gently roll the pup on his back and hold it for 30 seconds.

Struggles fiercely, flails, bites 1

Struggles fiercely, flails. 2

Settles, struggles, settles with eye contact 3

Slight struggle, then settles 4

No struggle, tail tucked 5

No struggle, strains to avoid eye contact 6

Social Dominance

Purpose: Degree of acceptance of human social dominance. How "forgiving" the pup is.

Method: Pup sits facing tester at a 45° angle. Tester strokes pup and puts his/her face close to pup.

Jumps, paws, bites, growls 1

Jumps, paws, licks. 2

Cuddles up to tester, tries to lick face 3

Sits quietly, accepts petting, nudges/licks hands. 4

Rolls over, no eye contact. 5

Goes away and stays away 6

151

Table 13-1   Puppy Aptitude Test (cont.)

Test and Purpose	Score	Comments
Elevation Dominance *Purpose:* Degree of accepting dominance while in position of no control. *Method:* Cradle the pup under its belly, fingers interlaced, and elevate just off ground for 30 seconds.	Struggles fiercely, bites. . . . . .1 Struggles . . . . .2 No struggle, relaxed, tail wags . . . . . . .3 No struggle, relaxed . . . . .4 No struggle . . . . .5 No struggle, frozen, tail/rear legs tense 6	
Retrieving (Obedience and Aptitude) *Purpose:* Degree of willingness to work with humans. High correlation between ability to retrieve and successful guide dogs, obedience dogs, and field trail dogs. *Method:* Attract pup's attention with crumpled paper ball. When he is watching, toss paper 4 feet away. When pup goes after it back up 2 feet and encourage him to come back.	Chases object, picks it up and runs away. . . . . .1 Chases object, stands over it, does not return. . . . . .2 Chases object, picks it up and returns to tester. . . . . .3 Chases object, returns without object to tester. . . . . .4 Starts to chase, loses interest . . . . .5 Does not chase .6	

Touch Sensitivity

Purpose: Degree of sensitivity to touch.

Method: Take webbing of one front foot and press between finger and thumb lightly, gradually increasing pressure on a scale from 1-10. Stop as soon as the puppy shows discomfort.

9-10 counts before response 1

7-8 counts before response 2

5-6 counts before response 3

3-4 counts before response 4

1-2 counts before response 5

Sound Sensitivity

Purpose: Degree of sensitivity to sound.

Method: Place pup in center of testing area and make a sharp noise a few feet away. A large metal spoon struck sharply on a metal pan twice works well.

Locates the sound, walks toward it 1

Locates sound, barks 2

Locates sound, shows curiosity, walks toward it 3

Locates the sound 4

Cringes, backs off, hides 5

Ignores sound, shows no curiosity 6

Chase Instinct

Purpose: Degree of response to moving object; chase instinct.

Method: Tie a string around a towel and drag it in front of the puppy from left to right.

Looks, attacks, bites. 1

Looks, barks, tail up 2

Looks curiously, attempts to investigate 3

Looks, does not go forward, tail down 4

Runs away, hides 5

Ignores, shows no curiosity 6

153

Table 13-1 Puppy Aptitude Test (cont.)

Test and Purpose	Score	Comments
Stability *Purpose*: Degree of intelligent response to strange object. *Method*: Place pup in center of testing area. Closed umbrella is held 4 feet away and pointed perpendicular to the direction the pup faces. The umbrella is opened and set down so the pup can investigate.	Walks forward, tail up, bites..........1 Walks forward, tail up, mouths ....2 Walks forward, attempts to investigate.................3 Looks curiously, stays put ....4 Goes away, tail down, hides ....5 Ignores, shows no curiosity 6	*Note*: Puppies frequently startle upon seeing the umbrella open. Score pup's response after umbrella is set down.
Energy Level *Purpose*: Degree of physical energy. *Method*: Observe pup on the other subtests and score according to most frequent activity observed. Check with breeder for confirmation.	Continually runs, pounces, wiggles, paws .... High Mostly trots, occasionally runs, pounces, wiggles .... Medium Walks slowly, sits quietly, remains in position usually ....Low Stands rigidly, eyes roll, tail down, ears back................ Stress	

Invest in a large wire crate. Place the puppy in the crate whenever you are gone from the house *and* whenever you are preoccupied. The crate is a safe haven for your puppy while you are gone from home. Dogs are pack animals and they find security in their dens. Your puppy will not like being socially isolated while you are gone but will find comfort in the security of his crate. This is because puppies usually think of crates as their own personal dens. Additionally, the crate will keep your puppy from hurting himself (puppies are famous for chewing on electrical cords) and from damaging your property (puppies are also famous for chewing on sofas). Again, it is very important to remember to place your puppy in the crate whenever you are at home but are preoccupied.

Watch the puppy with eagle eyes whenever he is loose in the house. Soon you will learn to recognize when your puppy has the urge to relieve himself. Some puppies circle around and around just before eliminating. Other puppies sniff furiously just before eliminating. By watching closely, you will soon learn your puppy's individual body language. If you catch your puppy going in the house, you must interrupt this behavior immediately. Do this by either yelling "No!" or by clapping your hands together. Quietly pick him up and take him outside to the area you have designated as the doggy toilet area. Always use the same door. Once outside, wait until the puppy resumes his business, praise lavishly and promptly return to the house.

Maintain Your Puppy on a Regular Schedule.

Minimize your puppy's chances of making a mistake by predicting when he will need to relieve himself. Every young puppy will have to relieve himself at certain critical times. These critical times include: as soon as he awakens, whenever he finishes a meal and at the end of each play session. Don't forget to take your puppy outside as soon as you let him out of his crate—he was probably sleeping before you opened the door. Some very young puppies will need to go out in the middle of the night. You will often be able to sleep in later by remembering to take your puppy outside just before you retire. It is also important to remember to feed meals at the same time each day. Don't vary your schedule on the weekends.

Reward Good Behavior; Ignore Bad Behavior.

Your puppy is a pack animal and seeks your approval—be sure to praise him when he's been good.

Puppies do not understand the past tense; they can only understand the present tense. Therefore, it is important to catch your puppy "in the act." Please note that a puppy cannot comprehend why you would take him to a past mistake and scold him. He would simply assume that whenever you are home and there is a mess in the house, you will be angry. He will not understand that he created the mess—that was an action from the past.

Dogs are by nature clean animals and will not intentionally soil their dens. Therefore, if your puppy should soil his crate, do not be concerned. Simply ignore the accident and clean it up. After all, puppies are a lot of work!

Summary of Major Points

1. Don't permit your puppy to eliminate in the house.
   a. Avoid "paper training."
   b. Place your puppy in the crate whenever you cannot watch him closely.
   c. When you spy your puppy in the middle of an accident, interrupt him and take him outside.
2. Adhere to a schedule.
   a. Take your puppy out at all of the critical times.
   b. Feed your puppy regular meals.
3. Praise but don't scold.
   a. Lavishly praise your puppy when he's been good.
   b. Ignore accidents unless you catch your puppy in the act.

14

Infertility in the Bitch

INFERTILITY is defined as the inability to conceive or maintain a normal pregnancy. A bitch can be labeled as being infertile only after sound breeding management and male fertility have been firmly established. A large percentage of missed breedings are secondary to improper breeding management. Whenever breeding failure occurs, the stud dog's fertility should be tested. The best test of male fertility is the production of puppies. Preferably, males in question should sire a litter with another bitch within six months of breeding to a potentially infertile bitch. If a cause for infertility is to be identified in a bitch, the inability to conceive must be distinguished from early embryonic death and abortion.

This chapter will discuss many of the possible causes of infertility and means to diagnose those causes. Spontaneous abortion will also be discussed.

CAUSES OF INFERTILITY

Causes of infertility in the bitch are many and varied. They may be classified as infectious, hormonal, anatomical and miscellaneous.

157

Infectious

Infections of either the vagina or the uterus may prevent conception and/or maintenance of pregnancy.

A vaginal infection is referred to as vaginitis and is most often due to a bacterial infection. *Brucella canis* is only one of many bacteria that may cause vaginitis. Occasionally the herpes virus will cause vaginitis in some bitches. Puppy vaginitis is frequently noted in young bitches. Most puppies outgrow this condition when they reach puberty. Some bitches, however, have lifelong problems. Although antibiotics appear to effect a cure, the vaginitis usually recurs when medication is discontinued. In cases of chronic, recurrent vaginitis, cultures of the vaginal microflora should be taken. Herpes virus should also be sought when culturing a case of vaginitis. Most bitches with vaginitis will have a minor discharge and will lick at their vulva frequently.

Disease of the uterus may also cause infertility. The uterus is subject to many diseases, such as metritis and pyometritis. Refer to Chapter 11 for a detailed discussion of metritis. "Pyometritis" is the medical term for a bacterial infection of the uterus. It is seen frequently in older bitches. If the cervix of an affected bitch is open, a vaginal discharge will be evident. If the cervix is closed, no vaginal discharge will be evident. Most bitches with pyometritis are systemically ill and show a variety of signs. Some of the signs that may be seen are an increased thirst, increased urination, fever and anorexia. A diagnosis of pyometritis may be confirmed with radiographs and white blood cell counts. Radiographs of a bitch with pyometritis will often show a grossly enlarged uterus. The white blood cell counts from affected bitches are typically elevated well above normal. Pyometritis is usually treated by spaying the bitch. Sometimes hormone injections may be given to affected bitches. This will allow them to go on to whelp a litter. Such injections are not without risk and are not always successful. Any bitch that will no longer be used for breeding should be spayed in order to avoid pyometritis.

Hormonal

Hormones are chemical substances produced by glands that are located throughout the body. Several glands may be implicated in causing infertility in the bitch by producing abnormal amounts of

158

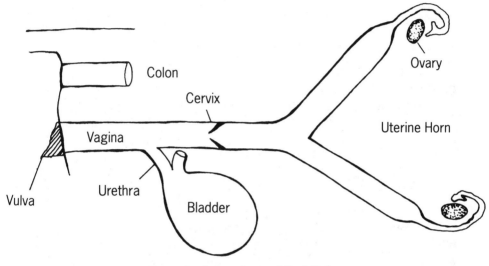

Colon

Cervix

Uterine Horn

Ovary

Vagina

Urethra

Bladder

Vulva

Reproductive anatomy of the bitch.

hormones. Offending glands may include the thyroid gland, the adrenal glands, the pancreas and the pituitary center.

Hypothyroidism is the most common hormonal cause of infertility in the bitch. Infertility may or may not be the only sign of hypothyroidism in affected bitches. Most hypothyroid bitches have an increased interestrous interval, which is defined as lasting twice the normal time between one proestrus and the next. Some hypothyroid bitches simply fail to cycle at all. Other hypothyroid bitches, however, may have normal estrous cycles and normal receptivity to males without conceiving. Signs evidenced by other body systems and the accurate diagnosis of hypothyroidism have been discussed elsewhere. Appropriate treatment with thyroid hormone replacement will allow some hypothyroid bitches to conceive. Litter size may be smaller than normal in such bitches.

The adrenal glands lie above each kidney and provide the body with a number of necessary steroidal hormones. If the adrenal glands malfunction, the steroidal hormones that they produce may interfere with the production of normal sex steroidal hormones. Reproductive signs are similar to those seen with hypothyroidism. Diseases of the adrenal glands, such as Cushing's and Addison's, are serious illnesses and usually negate the feasibility of breeding affected bitches.

The pancreas lies beneath the stomach. Part of the gland produces insulin, a hormone that regulates blood sugar levels. Diabetes, a disease that results from an inadequate production of insulin by the pancreas, may be caused by overproduction of other hormones in bitches that are not spayed. Therefore, affected bitches must be spayed.

The pituitary gland is a tiny gland located at the base of the brain that has a myriad of functions. One of these is to oversee the initiation of the estrous cycle. Therefore, disease of the pituitary may cause infertility in the bitch secondary to improper cycling.

Improper cycling may be evidenced by congenital anestrus, silent heats, split heats and ovulatory failures. Bitches with congenital anestrus never cycle. Bitches with silent heats lack outward signs of estrus. A split heat occurs when an affected bitch enters an estrous cycle only to have that estrus terminate and a second estrous cycle ensue about four weeks later. The second estrus is usually a normal, fertile estrus. Both silent and split heats are more commonly seen in young bitches. When a bitch fails to ovulate, eggs are not available for fertilization and progesterone is not produced to maintain a viable pregnancy. (Please note that cystic ovaries may also cause ovulatory failure.) Ovulatory failure can be diagnosed by measuring serum progesterone levels in affected bitches during an estrous cycle. It can sometimes be treated with appropriate hormone replacement.

Anatomical

Anatomical causes of infertility are not commonly seen but include vaginal strictures, intersex conditions, previous ovariohysterectomy and ovarian disease.

A thorough physical examination including a vaginal exam will reveal most vaginal strictures. Some strictures, however, are located beyond the reach of a vaginal exam. All strictures should be surgically severed. Most bitches with vaginal strictures are unwilling to be bred, and most male dogs will not persist in trying to breed them. Vaginal strictures are congenital but probably not hereditary.

Any time infertility is suspected, the possibility of a spay surgery by a previous owner must be excluded.

Intersex conditions are extremely rare and usually result from tightly inbred litters. Some are evident on physical examination because the bitch's clitoris is abnormally enlarged and phallic in appearance. Others are detected only through genetic analysis of chromosomes. All intersex conditions carry a very poor prognosis for future breeding potential.

Ovarian disease is probably the most common cause of anatomical infertility in the bitch. The ovaries are subject to developing both cysts and tumors. Most ovarian cysts and tumors cause estrus to be prolonged beyond the normal limit of twenty-one days. Some ovarian cysts, however, cause the interestrous interval to be decreased. Affected bitches, therefore, cycle more frequently than anticipated. Ovarian cysts can be definitively diagnosed only by exploratory surgery. They are sometimes treated effectively with hormonal injections. Alternately, they may be treated by drainage during exploratory surgery. Some ovarian cysts are caused by exogenous estrogen therapy. In such cases, the estrogen therapy must be discontinued. Tumors of the ovaries are occasionally seen in older bitches and must be treated by surgical removal.

Miscellaneous

A number of other, miscellaneous factors may adversely affect fertility in the bitch. Age has a direct effect on fertility. Bitches entering their first heat may miss because of a split heat. Young bitches may have silent heats. Beyond a certain age, time causes fertility to diminish.

The environment may also play a role in causing infertility. Stress is known to prevent embryo implantation and to cause fetal resorption. Many drugs have a negative effect on fertility.

Many systemic diseases may cause infertility. Liver disease is one example. When the liver is diseased, it does not degrade estrogen properly. The resultant elevation in estrogen levels may cause ovarian cysts to develop.

Psychological factors may also play a role in infertility. For example, some bitches adamantly refuse specific mates.

DIAGNOSING INFERTILITY

Diagnosing the cause of infertility in a bitch is often a challenge. A thorough physical examination with extra emphasis on the reproductive system will reveal some causes of infertility; a complete medical and reproductive history is necessary to define most causes. Often, ancillary tests are required to define a cause. Sometimes no cause can be identified.

Physical Examination

The physical examination of most bitches presented to a veterinarian for infertility is nonremarkable. If anything abnormal is noted, however, it could be clinically significant to the diagnosis of infertility. Signs of systemic disease should be especially noted. Such signs are nonspecific and might include a fever or hair loss, for example. Causes of infertility that might provide signs of a systemic nature include hypothyroidism, Cushing's disease, Addison's disease, diabetes, pyometritis, metritis, ovarian disease, liver disease and brucellosis. Abdominal palpation may reveal ovarian tumors. Vaginal strictures and intersex conditions may be discovered by visual examination of the reproductive tract.

History

A complete medical history will help to piece together shreds of evidence to indicate that a systemic disease may be the source of infertility.

A complete reproductive history should be obtained any time a bitch is suspected of infertility. If more than one person has owned the bitch, all owners must be questioned and all records collected. Records should include information on the age of onset of estrus, the frequency of estrous cycles, any breeding dates and their relation to the estrous cycle and information on previous litters, if any were produced.

An accurate history will allow infertile bitches to be classified into one of two categories: those bitches that cycle normally and those bitches that do not.

If a bitch appears to cycle normally but refuses to accept a male, a physical or a mental problem may exist. Vaginal strictures, for example, may be painful and cause a bitch to refuse a male. These strictures may or may not cause problems with whelping. If a bitch refuses a male for mere psychological reasons, she may be bred with artificial insemination.

If a bitch cycles normally and readily accepts the male yet fails to whelp a litter, she may not truly be infertile. She may conceive a litter but be unable to carry that litter to term. Early embryonic death is difficult to detect and, hence, probably occurs more often than is known. Definitive pregnancy diagnosis through the use of ultrasound will help to determine whether or not conception has occurred.

If conception has not occurred, it is important to utilize progesterone assays to determine whether ovulation has occurred. Progesterone assays are also helpful in determining whether progesterone levels remain high enough to maintain a pregnancy.

If a bitch appears to cycle normally, accepts a male readily and does not whelp a litter, she should be suspected of hormonal or uterine disease. The thyroid should be evaluated and uterine cultures taken.

Four different abnormalities may be noted in a bitch's estrous cycle. Some bitches simply fail to cycle. Some bitches have either an increased or a decreased interestrous interval. Other bitches suffer from a prolonged estrus.

Many problems may prevent a bitch from cycling at all. Bitches normally do not cycle until they reach puberty, which should occur within six months of her final growth. Most bitches begin cycling by twenty-four months of age. Bitches that have been spayed normally do not cycle. Several hormonal diseases, most notably hypothyroidism, may prevent a bitch from cycling normally. Intersex individuals may not cycle. Bitches occasionally have silent heats that go unnoticed. In addition, malnutrition will cause most bitches to stop cycling.

The interestrous interval is defined by the amount of time between one proestrus and the next. The interestrous interval is considered to be abnormally long if it is two times the average length of time. Older bitches gradually develop longer intervals of time between cycles. Some intersex individuals will cycle but will have abnormally long intervals. Hormonal diseases are probably the most common cause of an increased interestrous interval, and such an interval is the most common reproductive sign of hypothyroidism in the bitch.

A decreased interestrous interval is noted when a bitch fails to ovulate or has a split heat. A bitch may fail to ovulate because she has cystic ovaries. Some cysts appear spontaneously and others are caused by treatment with estrogenic hormones. As previously mentioned, the mismate shot is an injection of estrogen that may cause cystic ovaries.

Alternatively, cystic ovaries may cause a prolonged estrus. Estrus is defined as prolonged when it exceeds twenty-one days. Ovarian tumors may be present in aging bitches and may cause estrus to be prolonged. Liver disease may cause cystic ovaries, which may, in turn, cause estrus to be prolonged.

Laboratory Tests

Laboratory tests that can be used to aid a diagnosis of infertility include blood tests, vaginal cytology, uterine cultures, ultrasound and exploratory surgery.

The blood tests that are currently available include hormonal assays for thyroid hormone and progesterone levels and serology for brucellosis, herpes and toxoplasmosis infections. Brucellosis and hypothyroidism should be eliminated from the list of differential diagnoses in any infertile bitch.

Vaginal cytology is useful in establishing that a bitch is cycling normally and that proper breeding management is employed. Please refer to Chapter 8 for further information on vaginal cytology.

Cultures taken indirectly from the anterior vagina or directly from the uterus can be helpful in both diagnosing and treating infertility. Unfortunately, cultures are difficult to obtain and to interpret. A long cotton swab may be placed into the vagina to obtain a culture from the anterior vagina. However, bacteria found in the vagina may or may not represent the same bacteria present within the uterus. Additionally, microorganisms found in the vagina of bitches may simply be normal inhabitants and not a true cause of disease. A swab generally cannot be maneuvered through the cervix of a bitch to reach the uterus. Therefore, uterine cultures must be taken during an exploratory surgery. Some microorganisms, such as mycoplasma, ureaplasma and chlamydia, are suspected of causing uterine disease but are difficult to culture because they require special nutrients and environmental conditions to survive outside the uterus.

Ultrasound may be used to identify ovarian disease, to definitively diagnose pregnancy and to evaluate fetal viability. Unfortunately, ultrasound is not widely available. Sometimes simple radiology may substitute for ultrasound. Such is the case for some ovarian tumors and late-term fetal deaths.

Exploratory surgery under general anesthesia is often the final means used to diagnose infertility. As already noted, the uterus may be cultured during an exploratory. Ovarian cysts may be detected and surgically drained if medical treatment with hormones previously failed to help an affected bitch. Ovarian tumors may be noted and surgically removed. Most bitches with ovarian tumors must be simultaneously spayed. Finally, an anatomical abnormality, such as a vaginal stricture, may be identified and treated during an exploratory surgery.

ABORTION

Abortion is defined as the premature termination of a pregnancy. Diagnosis of the cause of an abortion is the same as for other problems with infertility—with one exception. The exception is that an aborted fetus may provide an opportunity to definitively diagnose a cause. Any aborted fetus should be saved for further examination by a veterinarian so that tissues may be cultured.

Causes of abortion, like causes of infertility, are many and varied. They include both fetal and maternal disorders.

Developmental defects of a fetus that are incompatible with life may cause the fetus to be aborted. Most of these defects are genetic in origin. It is possible for a bitch to abort defective fetuses and carry other, normal fetuses to term. Radiographs taken during the first trimester of pregnancy may have adverse effects on developing fetuses and may cause abortion to result.

Hormonal diseases, such as hypothyroidism and premature leuteolysis, may cause abortion. Hypothyroidism as a cause of abortion in the bitch is presumed. Premature leuteolysis prevents the affected bitch from producing enough progesterone to maintain a normal pregnancy.

Malnutrition due to calorie deprivation and various vitamin deficiencies has caused abortion in dogs. Hence, proper nutrition is imperative to successful reproduction.

Although trauma during pregnancy is occasionally suspected of causing an abortion, such occurrences are rare.

Many infectious agents, such as *Brucella canis*, other bacterial organisms, herpes virus, distemper virus and toxoplasmosis, may cause abortion. Inciting bacteria may be cultured from the uterus or from aborted material. Blood tests are available to detect herpes virus and toxoplasmosis.

Some drugs have been implicated in causing abortions. Dexamethasone injections and estrogens are used to intentionally interrupt a pregnancy.

Superfetation is defined as the presence of fetuses of different ages within the uterus during a given pregnancy. It has never been documented in the dog and is therefore not a possible cause of abortion.

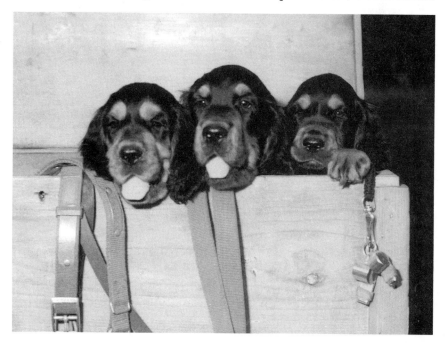

Ruth Genter

15

Male Infertility

INFERTILITY IN THE MALE DOG is defined as the inability to sire puppies. Breeding management should be closely scrutinized if a male readily breeds a bitch and fails to produce puppies. Improper timing may be the culprit rather than infertility.

Although most infertile dogs breed normally, some will refuse to breed. If a male refuses to breed a bitch, he has a psychological reason for doing so. He may have pain that inhibits his desire to breed a bitch, he may simply be insecure or he may ascertain that the bitch is not well. Although males exhibiting a pain reflex may not be collected, insecure males may be collected for artificial insemination. The general health of a bitch should be evaluated whenever an experienced stud dog discriminately refuses to breed her.

Other situations indicate that the general health and fertility status of the bitch, rather than that of the stud, should be evaluated. For example, when a male dog is bred to several bitches within a short span of time and some bitches produce puppies while others do not, the problem may be with the bitch and not the stud.

If, however, a male breeds several bitches within a short span of time and none of them conceive, his fertility should be evaluated. It is important to note that it takes approximately sixty-four days for sperm to mature within the canine reproductive tract. Therefore, any insult to sperm production may not be immediately evident. An infertile male may sire many litters a few months before infertility affects his production.

This chapter will discuss the diagnosis and common causes of infertility recognized in the male dog.

DIAGNOSIS OF INFERTILITY

Although the diagnosis of male infertility can be challenging, it is not necessarily an impossible task. To thoroughly investigate the cause of infertility in a male dog, adequate diagnostics are needed. Required are a thorough physical examination, a complete medical history and ancillary laboratory tests, as dictated by the physical exam and history.

Physical Examination

A general physical examination should be performed on any dog suspected of infertility in order to rule out anatomical causes. A thorough physical examinaton will reveal many musculoskeletal causes of infertility. A more detailed examination of reproductive organs is indicated when infertility is suspected. The penis should be extruded from its sheath to reveal any disease states. The testes, tubes and inguinal canals should be thoroughly and gently palpated to uncover any anatomical defects. Finally, the prostate should be examined by both rectal and abdominal palpation. If the prostate gland is painful, it is diseased.

Medical History

While the physical examination is being performed, a complete medical history should be taken. A general medical history includes information regarding appetite, vomiting, diarrhea, thirst, urinary habits, coughing, lameness, previous drug therapy and general attitude.

A specific reproductive history should also be taken. All information should be recorded, as it may prove to be significant. Required reproductive history includes age at first breeding, general breeding management practices, overall libido, dates bitches were bred and their relation to the bitch's cycle, manner of breeding (noting any outside ties and artificial inseminations), whether or not

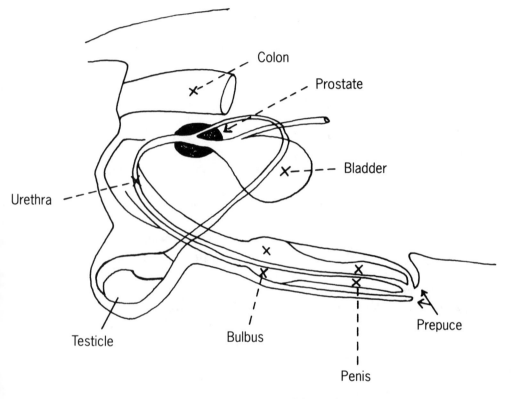

Colon

Prostate

Bladder

Urethra

Testicle

Bulbus

Penis

Prepuce

Reproductive anatomy of the male.

the dog incurred any trauma during breeding and results of brucellosis tests. A thorough history will often reveal that suspected cases of male infertility can be attributed to improper breeding management.

Laboratory Testing

Any dog with an infertility problem that shows no abnormalities on physical examination or deficits in breeding management should have three tests performed: a brucellosis test, thyroid hormone evaluation and semen analysis. Both brucellosis and hypothyroidism have been discussed elsewhere.

Semen analysis includes three separate parts: culture of the spermatic fraction, culture of the prostatic fluid and sperm analysis. Both the spermatic fraction and the prostatic fluid should be collected and cultured. Semen can be collected in three separate fractions. The second is the spermatic fraction and the third is the prostatic fraction. By culturing the sperm and the prostatic fluid, any bacterial infections of the testicles or the prostate will be identified. Special culture media are available to test for mycoplasmas, ureaplasmas and herpes virus if any of these diseases are suspected.

Additionally, a thorough sperm analysis should be performed. This analysis includes evaluation of three parameters: motility, morphology and total number of sperm.

To evaluate motility, a drop of semen is placed on a slide and examined under a microscope. Motility should be evaluated on semen kept at body temperature because a drop in temperature will inhibit sperm motility. Only sperm that have a progressive, forward pattern of movement should be considered motile. Normal semen samples will have at least 70 percent motility.

Once the sperm cells have been examined for motility, they can be stained and reevaluated under the microscope to detect any physical abnormalities. While the morphology of individual sperm cells is being evaluated, the types and relative numbers of physical abnormalities should be noted. All semen samples will contain some deformed sperm cells. The deformities become significant only if the relative number and type are important.

Finally, the total number of sperm per ejaculate should be determined. This number is actually a mathematical calculation based on the volume of semen ejaculated multiplied by the number of sperm counted per volume of semen evaluated. The volume of

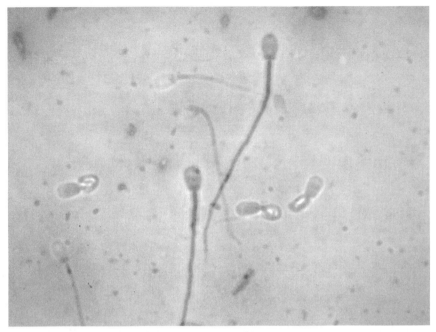

Normal microscopic appearance of canine sperm cells.

International Canine Genetics, Inc.

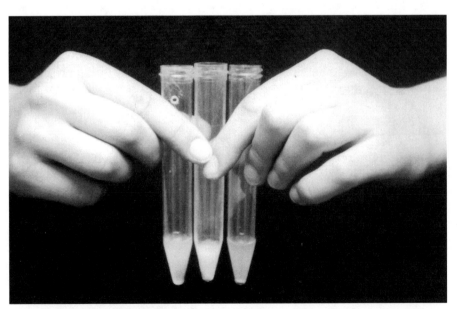

Canine semen is ejaculated in three fractions. The second, milky-white fraction contains the sperm cells.

semen ejaculated is recorded at the time of the ejaculation. Then a sample of semen is evaluated to determine how many sperm are present in a fixed volume. These two values are multiplied together to produce the total number of sperm per ejaculate. This calculation is necessary because the volume of semen ejaculated is variable. Some dogs ejaculate only 1 milliliter of semen, while others ejaculate as much as 25 milliliters of semen. Regardless of the volume of semen ejaculated, the sample should contain at least 200 million sperm per ejaculate for the male to have normal fertility.

Other diagnostic tests may become necessary to properly diagnose male infertility. Systemic diseases may be discovered with a complete blood count and/or blood chemistry panel. Diseases of the urinary tract may be discovered with a urinalysis and/or abdominal radiographs. Radiographs are useful in determining whether or not stones are present anywhere in the urinary tract. They are also useful in detecting an enlargement of the prostate gland. On rare occasions, the os penis—a long, thin bone located within the penis of the male dog—may be fractured. If fractured, it will be evident on a radiograph and will cause the dog to be a reluctant breeder. Hormonal assays occasionally prove useful. Testicular biopsies are sometimes needed to definitively diagnose male infertility.

CAUSES OF INFERTILITY

Causes of male infertility can be classified as inflammatory, hormonal, anatomical and environmental.

Inflammatory

Inflammation of any part of the male reproductive tract can cause infertility. Most inflammatory diseases result from bacterial infections and affect either the testicles or the prostate gland. Often, affected dogs experience too much pain to achieve an erection. If an affected dog can be collected for a semen analysis, both his motility and his sperm count may be below normal. Some inflammatory diseases, such as brucellosis, cause abnormal sperm morphology. Inflammation of the bladder can also cause infertility.

Inflammation of the testicles is termed orchitis. Orchitis is obvious because one or both of the testicles are grossly enlarged and painful. Affected dogs are reluctant to sit on their haunches and walk with a stilted gait. Orchitis can result from many primary causes. Brucellosis and hypothyroidism are among the many systemic diseases that may cause orchitis. The scrotal skin that covers the testicles is very sensitive and is easily traumatized. If the scrotal skin becomes irritated, it may affect the underlying testicles. Hence, caution should be used when choosing bedding materials and when bathing male dogs. Occasionally, a rubber band is found around the spermatic cord. In such cases, the damage is usually irreparable. No matter what the cause, the prognosis for future breeding potential of dogs with orchitis is guarded. In some dogs, eventual castration is necessary.

Inflammation of the prostate is termed prostatitis. Signs of prostatitis include bloody urine, difficulty urinating and difficulty passing bowel movements. These signs result because the prostate gland lies between the colon and the urethra. Many affected dogs are febrile. Most affected dogs are older. Prostatitis is usually caused by an ascending infection from the tip of the penis. However, brucellosis and other systemic infections may cause prostatitis. Some cases of prostatitis are effectively treated with antibiotics, although castration may eventually be needed.

Inflammation of the bladder is termed cystitis. Since the urinary and the reproductive tracts of the male dog join together in the urethra, disease of one system may affect the other system. Causes of cystitis are many and varied. Bacteria may ascend from the penis to infect the bladder. Systemic infections sometimes localize within the bladder. Metabolic diseases often cause the formation of crystals within the bladder, which then predispose the bladder to infections. Such crystals are rough and swirl within the bladder, causing irritation and allowing the surface to become infected.

Many types of crystals may be found in the urine of dogs. Dalmatians are infamous for forming urate crystals because of their unique metabolism of purine-type proteins. Some dogs, most notably Miniature Schnauzers, are born with a portal-caval shunt located within the liver. This shunt causes metabolic alterations that also predispose them to the formation of urate crystals. Any breed of dog may form struvite crystals.

To further complicate matters, bladder infections themselves may predispose dogs to develop crystals. This is because the infection alters the acidity of the urine and allows for more rapid crystallization.

Obviously, the treatment of cystitis depends upon discovering any underlying metabolic diseases and treating accordingly. Likewise, prognosis for future breeding potential depends upon the underlying cause. Dogs with metabolic diseases are likely to pass on these inherited tendencies and should not be bred. Dogs with a simple ascending infection are often treated effectively with antibiotics and urinary acidifiers.

Hormonal

Three hormonal diseases are known to cause infertility in male dogs: hypothyroidism, diabetes and hypogonadism.

Hypothyroidism is the most common hormonal cause of infertility in male dogs. It may cause a loss of libido and it invariably causes a decrease in sperm count and motility. The only sign of hypothyroidism in affected dogs may be infertility. Although infertile dogs may return to normal fertility with appropriate hormone replacement, the return may take several months.

Diabetes will cause decreased sperm counts in affected stud dogs. Other signs of diabetes, however, are usually more obvious. Diabetic dogs classically drink a lot of water, urinate large quantities of urine, eat voraciously and lose weight rapidly in spite of the increased appetite. Affected dogs must be treated with daily insulin injections and strict dietary management. No one knows whether or not fertility will return to normal after the diabetes is appropriately treated.

Hypogonadism is a poorly understood disease that is evidenced by a decrease in one or more of the sex hormones. Affected dogs usually have a normal libido but a marked decrease in sperm count and poor motility. The diagnosis is presumptive and treatment is usually unrewarding.

Anatomical

A number of anatomical abnormalities may cause infertility in male dogs. Some are congenital, some are hereditary and others are acquired.

Two congenital malformations may prevent the male dog from functioning normally. The first is a persistent penile frenulum; the other is phimosis. A persistent penile frenulum is a tag of skin that remains attached from the prepucial sheath to the penis. It must be surgically severed to allow for a normal erection. Phimosis is a defect

174

in the prepucial sheath that causes the opening to be too small to allow the penis to extrude from the sheath. This condition, too, must be surgically corrected.

Bilateral cryptorchids are sterile. Unilateral cryptorchids are not sterile but should not be bred, because cryptorchidism is believed to be inherited as a simple, recessive trait. Unlike many other mammalian species, dogs are not born with their testicles in the scrotal sac. Rather, the testicles descend into the sac sometime after birth.

Normal male puppies should have two intrascrotal testicles by the time they are sixteen weeks old. Occasionally puppies are encountered that do not drop their testicles into the scrotal sac until six months of age. No one knows for certain whether or not these late developers are truly normal. Cryptorchid testicles have a much higher incidence of disease than do normal testicles and are more likely to develop tumors. They are more likely to twist on themselves, a condition known as testicular torsion. Affected dogs are usually stiff-gaited and have abdominal pain. Testicular torsion is a medical emergency and may cause death if not treated rapidly with castration.

Paraphimosis is a condition in which the penis cannot retract back into the protective prepucial sheath. This, too, is a medical emergency and must be treated immediately or the penis may become gangrenous. Most often, paraphimosis occurs in relation to sexual activity. It is often caused by hairs around the prepucial opening that lodge between the penis and the prepuce. The hairs must be removed and the penis must be deflated with cool water to allow for retraction of the penis back into its sheath.

Testicular tumors are commonly seen in older, intact male dogs. Several types may develop within the testicle. Some are detected by palpating the testicles and noting one or more lumps. Other tumors produce hormones and cause obvious systemic signs, such as hair loss and enlarged mammary glands. Castration is the only treatment.

Environmental

Several environmental factors can have adverse effects on the fertility of stud dogs.

Many different drugs have negative effects on sperm production. Excessive use of steroids will decrease sperm count and may decrease libido. Drugs used to treat cancer patients will also decrease sperm count. However, numerous reproductive studies have refuted claims that diethylcarbamazine adversely affects fertility.

High environmental temperatures may also decrease sperm production. Heavily coated dogs are most susceptible to hyperthermia during the summer months. Infertility may sometimes be reversed with a change in the temperature.

Improper breeding management has also been implicated in causing male infertility. A male may be used daily for up to one week, if necessary. However, a male should not be used more often than every other day for any extended period of time.

Stress is an ill-defined factor that may adversely affect the health of dogs in many ways. It is often suspected to cause reproductive failure.

Hockenberry

PART THREE

Managing a Healthy Kennel

EVERY KENNEL MANAGER strives to see that the dogs he or she keeps are healthy. Unfortunately, dogs are biological creatures and, as such, are subject to a multitude of maladies. Proper management practices can prevent many of these maladies. Infectious diseases can be prevented by proper vaccination programs. Likewise, parasitic infections can be controlled when properly treated. Not all diseases can be prevented, however. When disease occurs in a kennel, it is best managed by early detection and intervention. Kennel managers should establish administrative policies to reach the objective of maintaining a kennel full of healthy dogs.

16

Preventing Infectious Disease

ROUTINE VACCINATION programs provide the cornerstone to preventive veterinary care. Currently vaccines are available to protect dogs against six viral and three bacterial diseases. The six viral diseases are distemper, hepatitis, parainfluenza, parvovirus, coronavirus and rabies. The three bacterial diseases are leptospirosis, *bordetella bronchiseptica* and Lyme disease. This chapter will discuss types of vaccines, routes of vaccine administration and vaccination protocols. Individual infectious diseases for which vaccines are available will also be discussed.

TYPES OF VACCINES

Vaccines prepared to prevent viral diseases are either modified-live virus (MLV) or killed vaccines. It is important to distinguish between the two products. MLV products actually live and reproduce within the dog in order to stimulate an immune response. The viruses that live and reproduce are considered avirulent. This means that they are not considered to be capable of producing active, clinical disease in healthy dogs. They should never be given to pregnant or debilitated dogs, as clinical disease may result from vaccination of these dogs. MLV vaccines are generally considered to provide a stronger protection than the killed viral vaccines.

Vaccines prepared to prevent bacterial diseases are killed products referred to as bacterins. They stimulate a weak immune response and are often only considered effective for six months. Most adverse vaccine reactions are attributed to the bacterin components of a vaccine.

ROUTES OF ADMINISTRATION

Three routes are commonly used to administer vaccines: subcutaneous (SC), intramuscular (IM) and intranasal. Both SC and IM vaccines may be accidentally administered into a blood vessel and then cause an anaphylactic reaction. Thus, it is important to draw back on the plunger of the syringe to ensure that no blood fills the hub of the needle before injecting a vaccine.

Anaphylactic reactions usually occur within ten minutes and require immediate veterinary care. Milder allergic reactions may occur within twenty-four hours after a vaccine is administered. They usually cause tremendous facial swelling and should be cared for by a veterinarian. Laymen should not administer vaccines to dogs that have had vaccine reactions; a veterinarian should vaccinate these dogs.

Subcutaneous vaccines are given anywhere loose folds of skin abound. Usually, they are given along the back of the neck or in the flank region. IM vaccines may be given along the back to either side of the vertebral column or in the back of the thigh. Some manufacturers specifically indicate that a product must be administered IM in the caudal thigh. It is important to note that the sciatic nerve runs along the back of the thigh and must be avoided when giving injections into the caudal thigh. If an injection is given into the sciatic nerve, the leg may become permanently paralyzed.

Intranasal vaccines are sprayed directly into the nostrils. They generally give a more rapid response because they stimulate a local respiratory immunity as well as a systemic immunity.

180

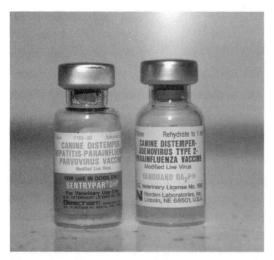

Many combination vaccines are currently available. Some also include parvovirus vaccine (Sentrypar DHP, Beecham, and Vanguard DA$_2$P, Norden).

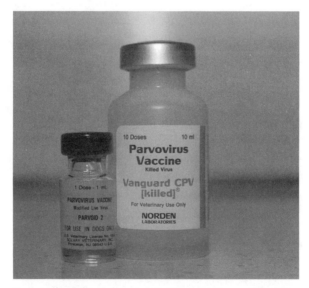

Parvovirus vaccine is available in both modified live and killed virus formulations (Parvoid 2, Solvay, and Vanguard CPV, Norden).

VACCINATION PROTOCOLS

Puppies are traditionally vaccinated at six, nine and twelve weeks of age with a combination vaccine that is boostered annually. The combination vaccine protects against distemper, hepatitis, leptospirosis, parainfluenza and parvovirus and is referred to as a DHLPP booster.

A rabies vaccine is usually given at three months of age with the last DHLPP and should always be boostered in one year. Subsequent rabies boosters may be given at various intervals. Although some rabies vaccines are licensed for only one year of protection, most are licensed for three years. State laws, however, vary tremendously in their requirements. State or local authorities should be contacted to find out what any given residency requires. If a dog is at a high risk of contacting rabid wildlife, it should be vaccinated annually with a three-year vaccine. This will afford maximum protection.

A relatively new combination vaccine is available that includes coronavirus. It usually excludes leptospirosis. Many veterinarians use this and similar products lacking leptospirosis as an initial combination vaccine booster so that very young puppies are not subjected to the possibility of having a bacterin reaction. The manufacturer recommends that two initial boosters be followed by an annual booster.

Another combination vaccine often given for initial protection of very young puppies is the distemper/measles vaccine. It is given to provide extra protection against distemper infection. The human measles virus is very similar to the canine distemper virus. Thus, when a puppy is vaccinated against human measles, that puppy

Table 16-1
Sample Vaccination Protocol

Age in weeks	Vaccine given
6	DA2PL
8	Parvo
10	DA2PL
12	Parvo
14	DA2PL
16	Rabies
18	*Bordetella*
20	Parvo

makes antibodies that protect it against canine distemper. However, the human measles vaccine may cause an allergic reaction in some dogs.

Several brands of yet another combination vaccine, referred to as DA2PL, are available. This combination excludes parvovirus. Many breeders and some veterinarians prefer to use separate DA2PL and parvovirus vaccines rather than a DHLPP. These vaccines are given separately to prevent distemper infection. Some people believe that the parvovirus component of DHLPP vaccines will suppress the immune system of some puppies. Once the immune system is suppressed, the distemper component may infect inoculated puppies. Separating the parvovirus vaccine from the distemper vaccine is strongly recommended.

Dobermans and Rottweilers seem to be genetically predisposed to acquiring parvovirus. Hence, most veterinarians recommend giving additional parvo boosters to these puppies and to other puppies at high risk of contacting parvovirus. The last booster should be given to these puppies at or after twenty weeks of age.

Bordetella vaccines may be given to puppies as young as two weeks of age to protect against kennel cough. The vaccine should be boostered at least once each year.

A vaccine against Lyme disease is now available.

DISTEMPER

The development of a vaccine against distemper was one of the greatest advances in canine preventive medicine. Almost invariably fatal, this once-prevalent disease is rarely seen now. The few dogs that survive distemper may have discolored teeth, hardened pads and/or neurological tics. Distemper brings to mind a picture of an afflicted puppy with severe diarrhea and profuse discharge from the eyes and nostrils. With time, classically infected puppies go on to develop neurological signs shortly before dying.

Unfortunately, distemper has also been confirmed in vaccinated puppies. These puppies never show the initial, classical signs of distemper. Rather, they present to the veterinarian with neurological signs.

A well-vaccinated, five-month-old Puli puppy once presented an interesting case. On the day that she was brought to the emergency room, she had gotten herself caught behind a radiator. In order to free the puppy, the owner actually had to remove the radiator from the floorboards. Prior to that day, the Puli had been acting somewhat odd. She would not walk freely through a room but, rather, meandered along the baseboards. She chewed incessantly and seemed to prefer metal objects. Physical examination revealed that she was blind and had other neurological deficits. Lead poisoning was suspected since the house had old paint on the radiators. However, her blood lead levels were found to be normal. Distemper virus was eventually found in her central nervous system. Obviously, there had been a break in the vaccine. Perhaps the vaccine had not been stored or administered properly. Perhaps the maternal antibodies were so high that she never mounted a response to the vaccines.

A growing number of people are concerned that the very nature of combined vaccines may be the source of distemper infections in "adequately" vaccinated puppies. As previously mentioned, they believe that the portion of the vaccine that contains MLV parvo may immunosuppress puppies and allow the portion of the vaccine that contains MLV distemper virus to infect these puppies.

The only way to avoid this possible problem is to administer the distemper vaccine and the parvo vaccine separately. The distemper vaccine should be given two weeks before the parvo vaccine. All available distemper vaccines are MLV, but parvo vaccines may be either MLV or killed products. Again, although MLV products provide a stronger immunity, killed products are safer.

PARVOVIRUS

Unlike distemper, parvovirus is still commonly seen. Any one who has nursed puppies infected with parvo will never forget the classic signs. Affected puppies have severe bloody diarrhea and bloody vomiting. Although they never spike a fever, blood tests usually show a marked drop in the number of circulating white blood cells. This drop in the number of white blood cells makes affected puppies inclined to develop other infections. Although the mortality is not as great for puppies affected with parvovirus as it is for puppies affected with distemper, recovery requires intensive care. Many puppies with parvovirus are euthanized simply because their owners cannot afford treatment. Fortunately, many treated puppies survive. The disease is prevalent among urban and show environments. Im-

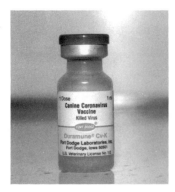

A killed coronavirus vaccine is widely available. Modified live virus versions of coronavirus vaccine were found to cause many undesirable side effects and are no longer on the market (Duramune Cv-K, Fort Dodge Laboratories).

All rabies vaccines are killed products. Some may be given subcutaneously; others may be given only intramuscularly into the caudal thigh (Imrab, Pitman-Moore, and Rabcine-3, Beecham):

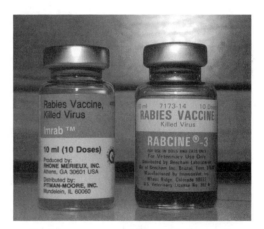

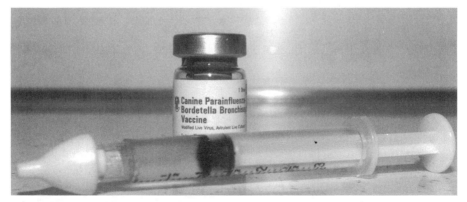

Many kennel cough vaccines are administered intranasally (Intra-Trac II, Schering Corporation).

munizations against parvovirus should continue until puppies are at least five months old if they are at risk of contacting parvovirus.

CORONAVIRUS

Great controversy exists as to whether coronavirus causes a significant amount of disease in dogs in this country. Because no one knows just how significant this disease is, no one knows just how important it is to vaccinate against it. Different geographical regions seem to have greater or lesser problems with coronavirus; thus a veterinarian should be consulted when considering whether to vaccinate against it. Currently, only a killed vaccine is available. A number of years ago, a MLV vaccine was produced and marketed for a short while. Veterinarians quickly discovered that it caused a lot of illnesses. Most of the vaccine reactions were much more serious than coronavirus itself. No similar problems have been encountered with the newer, killed product.

PARAINFLUENZA

Most combination vaccines manufactured today contain a MLV parainfluenza-2 component. This component simultaneously protects dogs against two very different diseases. One is infectious canine hepatitis. The other is a variant of kennel cough. Years ago vaccines were made with a parainfluenza-1 component. This component frequently reverted to an active, infectious form and caused a condition known as blue eye. Parainfluenza-1 is no longer used in combination vaccines because of this problem.

RABIES

MLV rabies vaccines are no longer available because the risk of having a break in the vaccine is too great. Only killed rabies vaccines are available today.

Rabies is invariably fatal and it still exists in this country. Vaccination requirements vary from state to state. County authorities should be consulted to find out what local laws apply to licensing and rabies vaccination. When showing dogs in Canada, it is important to inquire about both American and Canadian laws long before an expected departure date. The laws are not only confusing, they are also rigid. Currently, an owner will not be permitted to reenter the United States if his dog was vaccinated less than one month before their reentry date.

Although the laws might seem to be unreasonable, they serve a good purpose. Rabies exists in many populations of wild animals in this country and will continue to spread unabated. The only buffer between wild, rabid animals and humans is the population of domestic animals. If domesticated animals are vaccinated, they are protected and so are the people who contact them.

Many people have a fallacious mental image of the rabid dog. Although some rabid dogs become vicious, many do not. One of my colleagues performed a Caesarean section on a Beagle bitch that was rabid. Obviously, she did not know that the Beagle was rabid when she performed the surgery. The dog survived the C-section and went home to nurse her litter of six puppies while eating and otherwise acting relatively normal. When she suddenly died, my colleague was concerned enough to request a postmortem exam. When the exam showed nothing unusual, my concerned colleague phoned the owner to tell him the results. In the course of the conversation, she discovered that the Beagle had bitten her owner in a natural display of maternal protection. The only reason that the dog was discovered to be rabid was because my colleague was so dedicated and conscientious. When the owner refused to take a specimen of brain tissue to the laboratory for testing, the veterinarian drove more than an hour each way to deliver the specimen herself on her day off. Many exposed people were quite thankful that she was so dedicated.

LEPTOSPIROSIS

Leptospirosis is another disease that has a reservoir in wild animals. It is a disease that affects the liver and kidneys; affected animals shed the bacteria in their urine, which usually contaminates drinking water. Deer appear to perpetuate the disease in sylvan areas, while rats appear to perpetuate the disease in urban areas. Fortunately, the disease is relatively uncommon. As mentioned previously, the bacterin used to protect dogs from leptospirosis may cause vaccine reactions and may only be effective for six months.

187

BORDETELLA

Bordetella causes infectious tracheobronchitis, or kennel cough, in dogs. *Bordetella bronchiseptica* is a bacterium and usually acts in concert with one or more viruses, such as the parainfluenza virus, to cause kennel cough.

Signs are classic. Affected dogs have a dry hack, often making owners believe that the dogs have something caught in their throats. The disease seldom causes permanent problems but can persist for weeks and is highly contagious among dogs housed together. Affected dogs should be treated with antibiotics and cough suppressants to hasten recovery.

An intranasal vaccine has been developed that provides for excellent immunity. It contains both a *Bordetella* bacterin and a MLV parainfluenza component, and it affords rapid immunity. One manufacturer even recommends using it in the face of an infection to hasten recovery. It is safe enough to use in two-week-old puppies. The manufacturer recommends annual boosters. Dogs at high risk, however, should be boostered every six months, since the vaccine is composed of a bacterin. Although it is common practice to administer DHLPP and *Bordetella* vaccines simultaneously, one manufacturer does not recommend this practice.

17

Controlling Intestinal Parasites

INNUMERABLE PARASITES plague the digestive system of dogs. Fortunately, only a few of these parasites commonly affect American dogs. Intestinal parasites that are commonly seen include nematodes, or worms (roundworms, hookworms, whipworms and tapeworms), and protozoa (coccidia and *Giardia*).

Intestinal parasites are usually diagnosed by performing a fecal examination. A fresh sample of stool is mixed with a saturated solution that causes the parasitic eggs to float. These eggs can then be identified under a microscope.

A fecal examination will not detect all infections. Eggs produced by some parasites do not float well with standard solutions. Such is the case with tapeworm eggs and *Giardia* cysts. Additionally, eggs will not always be present in samples from infected dogs. If the sample if too old, eggs will disintegrate and the infection will not be found. Some parasites, such as whipworms, produce few eggs and produce them intermittently. Such infections may easily go undetected.

Although definitive diagnosis of some of these parasites can be difficult, medical treatment is usually safe and easy. Proper control of intestinal parasites, however, requires that both the dog and the environment be treated. Treating infected dogs without treating their environment is only a stopgap measure. Reinfection will occur if the environment is ignored. To prevent reinfection, a thorough understanding of the parasite's life cycle is needed.

ROUNDWORMS

Roundworms have adapted remarkably well to life with dogs and hence infect almost all puppies. In fact, it is estimated that 75 percent of all puppies in the United States are infected with roundworms. The life cycle of the dog roundworm is difficult to interrupt. Roundworms encyst in the muscles of adult dogs, who usually develop enough immunity to prevent active intestinal infections. However, when an adult bitch becomes pregnant, hormonal changes activate the dormant, encysted roundworms. The larvae (immature worms) then penetrate directly through the placenta and also into the bitch's milk and infect the puppies. Active worms living within the bitch's digestive system reproduce and shed eggs in the bitch's feces. These eggs reinfect both mother and puppies when they contact the infected feces. The eggs hatch into larvae, which leave the digestive tract and migrate along the dog's windpipe. The larvae are subsequently coughed up and swallowed, thus completing the cycle. There is no affordable treatment currently available to kill dormant cysts in adult bitches. This is why puppies are almost always born infected with roundworms; the complicated life cycle of the dog roundworm allows it to be ubiquitous.

Heavily burdened puppies have a classic appearance. They are potbellied and have dull, dry haircoats. Occasionally they will pass entire worms in the stools or even vomit entire worms. These worms resemble cooked spaghetti noodles.

Puppies can be safely treated for roundworms with pyrantel pamoate (Nemex) as early as two weeks of age. Retreatments are necessary to eliminate infection because the drug kills only adult worms within the digestive system. The dam should also be treated because she cleans the feces of the puppies. Empirical treatment of all puppies with pyrantel pamoate at two, four, six and eight weeks of age is recommended. This drug is available without a prescription.

It is unusual to find whole worms in the stools of puppies treated with pyrantel pamoate. This is because the drug kills the worms and the puppy's digestive tract then digests them. There are alternative

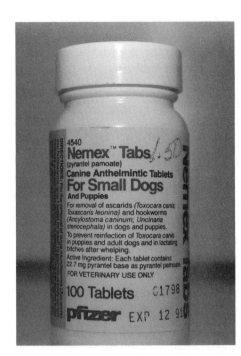

Pyrantel pamoate is an effective agent in the treatment of both roundworms and hookworms (Nemex, Pfizer).

Fenbendazole will treat roundworms, hookworms, whipworms and some tapeworms (Panacur, Hoechst-Roussel).

drugs that do not kill the worms. Rather, they merely paralyze the worms so that they release their hold on the intestinal wall. Since many whole worms may be passed after treatment with these drugs, impaction is a possible side effect and could be fatal.

Roundworm larvae are a public health threat to children. Every puppy buyer who has small children should be instructed to keep children away from the feces of puppies.

HOOKWORMS

Hookworms have also adapted well to life with dogs, but they are not usually as prevalent as roundworms. Some southern states have serious problems with hookworm infestations, however. Although hookworm larvae cannot penetrate the placenta of pregnant bitches, they can enter the milk of nursing bitches. Hence puppies can have active hookworm infections shortly after birth. Adult dogs do not develop any immunity to hookworms and may also have active infections.

Hookworms were named such because they have hooks within their mouths that cut into the intestinal wall. They have a nasty habit of moving from one site to another, leaving spots of bleeding intestinal wall behind. As a result, affected dogs often have bloody stools and anemia. Hookworms are too small to be seen in the stool with the naked eye. However, they may be evident in affected dogs because of the resultant bloody stools. Heavily infected puppies that are anemic have pale gums; they may die as a result of the anemia, if it is severe enough.

Treatment of puppies for hookworms is the same as for roundworms. Hookworm larvae found in the environment may be destroyed with a solution of ten pounds of sodium borate per one hundred square feet.

Hookworm larvae are also a public health threat to children. Children should be kept away from the feces of puppies.

WHIPWORMS

Whipworms, hookworms and roundworms are all transmitted by the "fecal-oral route." In other words, eggs are passed in the feces of infected dogs and are transmitted to other dogs when they,

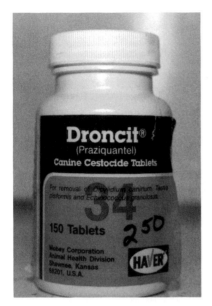

Praziquantel will eradicate both *Dipylidium caninum* and *Taenia pisiformis* (Droncit, Haver)

Sulfadimethoxine is one of the few drugs available to treat coccidia (Albon, Roche).

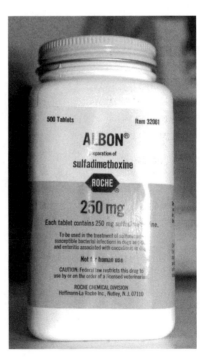

193

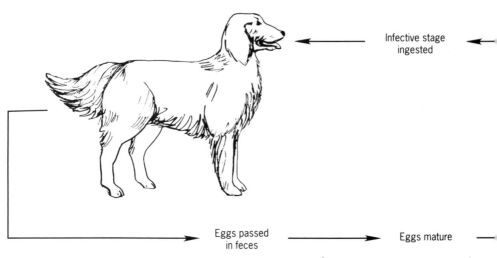

Fecal-oral route of transmission typical of roundworms, hookworms and whipworms.

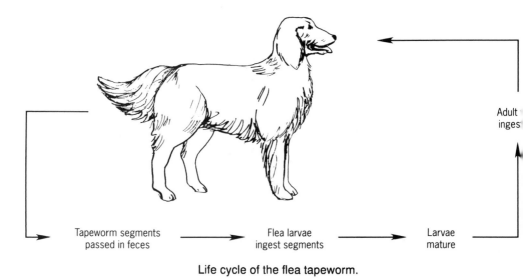

Life cycle of the flea tapeworm.

in turn, orally contact infected feces. Whipworm infection is fairly common in many geographical regions.

Whipworm eggs are essentially indestructible. Once a property is infected it basically remains so. If dogs cannot be removed from an infested property, they should be treated for whipworm infection at three-month intervals.

Recurrence is common, so treatment can be costly. Treatment can also be dangerous and painful. Some drugs cannot be given unless treated dogs are free from heartworm infection; others cannot be given with flea products. One of these drugs has caused liver disease in treated dogs. Several of these drugs cause pain and discomfort when injected. Fenbendazole (Panacur) is relatively safe and effective. It is available only through veterinary prescription.

Whipworm infections are usually difficult to detect. Adult whipworms reproduce and shed eggs intermittently. As a result, many infected dogs have negative fecal exams. Daily fecal exams were performed for six consecutive days before finding a single whipworm egg in a fecal sample of an infected bitch. Fortunately, this bitch had classic signs of a whipworm infection.

Whipworms do not cause classic signs in all dogs. Most affected dogs have excessive mucus in their stools. One local breeder notes that his dogs are "shedding their intestinal lining." This is not exactly accurate, but it is a common misconception. Whipworms live in the dog's colon, which is the very end of the digestive tract. The colon normally reabsorbs much of the water in a dog's feces and produces mucus to lubricate the relatively dry stools for easier passage. Affected dogs have loose feces and excessive mucus in their stools because the whipworms irritate the lining of the colon. Affected dogs may vomit because of the phenomenon known as the colonogastric reflex. Because of this reflex, irritaton of the colon induces vomiting of the stomach contents. Sometimes affected dogs may drag their behinds along the ground in an attempt to relieve their itching. Some affected dogs have blood in their stools.

There are no known public health threats caused by whipworm infection in dogs.

TAPEWORMS

Tapeworms cause marked weight loss in affected dogs. Many affected dogs scoot their behinds along the ground because emerging tapeworm segments make the anus itchy.

Although many different kinds of tapeworms can infect American dogs, only two kinds are common: *Dipylidium caninum* and *Taenia* spp. They are commonly referred to as the flea and the rabbit tapeworm, respectively.

Tapeworms have an indirect life cycle that is much more complicated than the direct life cycle of roundworms, hookworms and whipworms. The indirect life cycle of the tapeworm mandates that it pass through two hosts. The flea tapeworm requires both a dog and a flea as hosts. The rabbit tapeworm requires both a dog and a rabbit as hosts. In order to effectively treat dogs for tapeworms, the intermediate host—either the flea or the rabbit—must be eliminated. In other words, unless the flea problems are cleared or the rabbit populations decreased at the same time that the dog is medicated, reinfection is likely.

Only a few drugs effectively treat dogs for tapeworms. Some are effective against *Taenia* but not against *Dipylidium*. Currently, praziquantel (Droncit) and espiprantel (Cestex) are available to effectively combat common tapeworms. Praziquantel has been in use for many years and has a wide margin of safety. It is expensive, however. Espiprantel is a relatively new drug; reproductive studies were not completed at the time this was written. Both of these drugs are available only through veterinary prescription, and neither is effective against the other types of worms.

Rare cases of human infection with *Dipylidium* have been reported. Therefore, it is important to control flea problems.

COCCIDIA

Coccidia are single-celled organisms that inhabit the intestinal tract of animals. Coccidial infections are most commonly seen in young dogs and puppies. Overcrowding is thought to perpetuate the disease. Adult dogs can harbor a few of these organisms with no apparent ill effects. Puppies with coccidia usually have bloody diarrhea.

Treatment can be difficult. Only a few sulfa-type antibiotics are effective against coccidia. If the medication is not administered for an appropriate period of time, the infection may not clear. Some veterinarians treat for twenty-one consecutive days, although treatment for ten days is usually adequate. Recurrence is common.

As with whipworms, coccidia seem to infest a property. If there are problems with coccidia infections in one litter, subsequent litters are likely to be infected. To reduce the chances of subsequent infections with coccidia, future litters should be given a new environment. A new whelping box should be secured, a different run should be used and a different area of the yard should be fenced. Adult dogs, fortunately, seem to have some degree of immunity against obvious disease. However, some veterinarians prefer to treat all dogs on an infected property, both young and old.

GIARDIA

Giardia is another single-celled organism that infects the digestive system of dogs. It is transmissible to people. Many water supplies and lakes are reservoirs for *Giardia*. Signs of infection may be vague; intermittent diarrhea is a common symptom. Metronidazole is the only drug available to treat *Giardia*.

The heart of a dog that died of severe heartworm infestation. Note the large number of adult heartworms in this sample.

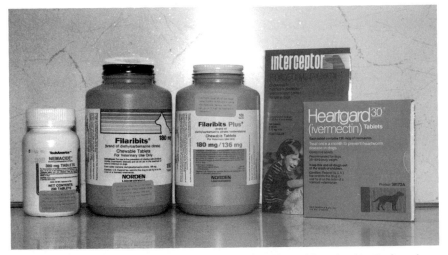

From the time heartworm became a national health problem for North American dogs, preventive medication has undergone numerous improvements. Today it is possible to obtain heartworm preventive medication in many highly efficacious forms.

18

Heartworm Prevention

HEARTWORMS are nematodes that live within the chambers of the heart. They look like spaghetti noodles and clog the chambers of the heart. Adult heartworms usually reproduce within the heart; resultant larvae are referred to as microfilariae. Microfilariae circulate within the bloodstream of infected dogs. They are transmitted when mosquitoes bite infected dogs, pick up microfilariae with their blood meal and then transmit the microfilariae when they bite other dogs.

Eventually heartworm infection leads to irreparable heart failure. Early detection and treatment is the only way to save infected dogs. Three tests are used to detect heartworm infection: the direct smear, the modified Knott's test and the occult test.

The direct smear is easy to perform. A small sample of blood is drawn and examined under the microscope. Microfilariae are transparent and difficult to see directly, but they are very active and are obvious because they cause red blood cells to swirl. Since only a drop of blood is examined, the concentration of microfilariae must be quite high in order to detect an infection; a direct smear may be negative if an infected dog has few microfilariae. Such is the case in early infections and in dogs that mount a large immune response against circulating microfilariae.

In order to better detect infections in dogs that have few circulating microfilariae, the modified Knott's test was developed. It uses a larger volume of blood; it is, therefore, a more sensitive test that detects a smaller concentration of microfilariae. A sample of blood is drawn from the suspected dog, mixed with a lysing solution to destroy red blood cells and then passed through a filter. The filter is then stained and examined under a microscope. The stain allows better visualization of the naturally transparent microfilariae. Although the test is more sensitive, it requires better technical skill in interpretation. This is because many extraneous fibers from the filter may be confused with the microfilariae, which are killed by the lysing solution and are no longer mobile.

The third test used to detect heartworm infection is the occult antibody or antigen test. Again, a sample of blood is drawn from the suspected dog. This sample is then tested with sophisticated techniques. Suffice it to say that if a dog is infected with heartworms, that dog should produce antibodies against the adult heartworms, and this test usually detects those antibodies. The occult test is the only accurate test for dogs that have no circulating microfilariae. Such is the case when dogs are infected with heartworms all of the same sex. The occult test is not accurate, however, for dogs that have large numbers of microfilariae because the antibodies will adhere to the microfilariae and not be detected by the test.

For routine annual screening of apparently healthy dogs, both the direct smear and the modified Knott's tests should be performed. For screening of dogs that are in endemic areas or that are highly suspect, the occult test and either the direct smear or the modified Knott's test should be done.

Most dogs infected with heartworms are diagnosed during routine annual physical examinations and vaccinations. At the time of the exam, most owners respond that their dogs are coughing but that they were not alarmed by the cough.

Occasionally a case of an occult heartworm infection is detected. In such cases the dog will have a history of coughing and abnormal chest radiographs. The direct smear and/or the Knott's tests will be negative. Such infections are confirmed by an occult antibody or antigen test. Occult heartworm infections are much more prevalent in endemic areas.

Two steps are usually required to treat dogs infected with heartworms. First, the adult heartworms must be killed. Thiacetarsamide (Caparsolate) is routinely used to kill adults. It is an arsenical drug that may cause severe side effects. Liver and kidney damage may result from treatment, and local tissue damage will result if the drug is not injected directly into a vein. Dogs must be hospitalized during treatment. Intravenous injections are given every twelve hours for a total of four injections. Dogs are closely monitored for complications, and treatment may be terminated if complications occur. Dogs must be kept quiet for at least a month after treatment with thiacetarsamide.

After the adults are killed and the dog is stable, any microfilariae must be killed. Many drugs are available to kill the microfilariae. Most may be given orally and may be dispensed at home.

Heartworm is a preventable disease. Three drugs are currently used to prevent dogs from acquiring active heartworm infections: diethylcarbamazine (DEC), ivermectin and milbemycin oxime.

DEC is an oral preventive medicine that is administered daily. It is quite safe for use in tested dogs. Untested dogs may have an anaphylactic reaction to DEC if they have circulating microfilariae. Although it is safe, DEC is inconvenient because it must be given daily and it is bitter. Highly palatable chewable forms are available. This drug may be packaged in combination with another drug; the purpose of adding it is to prevent infection with some intestinal parasites, although it may cause liver damage in some dogs. DEC may be used alone in both stud dogs and brood bitches with no ill effects; it is only available through prescription.

Ivermectin (Heartgard-30) is an oral preventive medicine that is administered once every thirty days. Heartgard-30 is the only product containing ivermectin that is currently approved by the Federal Drug Administration to prevent heartworm infection in dogs. It is available only through veterinary prescription.

Many people have used cattle or horse products containing ivermectin in dogs. Most of the time, these products can be easily obtained by laymen at feed stores or tack shops. These products may be extremely dangerous, as dosages administered from these products can be fatal. These products were developed for species much larger than even the largest dog. They were also intended to be given to large animal species at larger dosages. One Saluki bitch was hospitalized for days to treat liver failure after her owner dosed her with a cattle product. This breeder almost lost her foundation bitch.

Ivermectin does not eliminate circulating microfilariae at the dosage used to prevent heartworm infection. Therefore, the occult test is not recommended as a sole means of screening and detection

Mosquito bites
an infected dog

Microfilaria develop
within the mosquito

Same mosquito
bites another dog

Life cycle of the heartworm in dogs.

in dogs receiving ivermectin as a preventive. Much confusion has resulted because ivermectin can effectively remove circulating microfilariae from an infected dog; however, to do this it must be used at much higher dosages than that used for monthly prevention.

Milbemycin oxime (Interceptor) is also administered once each month to prevent heartworms. It may also be used to prevent hookworm infection. This drug is relatively new.

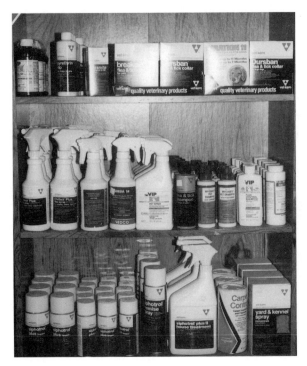

A great variety of preparations exist to control external parasites on dogs and in their surroundings. Before using any pesticide, read the label and follow the directions and cautions explicitly. Not all preparations are safe for certain categories of dogs.

Just as it is to every dog owner, the flea is at the top of every dog breeder's "hit list." Unfortunately, fleas are tough, resilient adversaries—a headache that won't disappear with aspirin.

19

Controlling External Parasites

$\mathbf{A}$S IS THE CASE with internal parasites, effective control of external parasites can only be achieved through an accurate identification of offending parasites and a thorough understanding of each parasite's life cycle.

Some external parasites, such as ticks, can be identified with the naked eye. Other parasites, such as mites, can only be identified with the aid of a skin scraping and microscopic examination. A veterinarian can perform skin scrapings easily and quickly.

Although some parasites only require one host, other parasites require several species of hosts. Some ticks, for example, require two or more species of hosts and cannot reproduce without both of these hosts.

Some external parasites, such as most lice and mites, spend all their lives on their host, the dog. These parasites have a simple life cycle that is easy to interrupt simply by treating the host. Other parasites, such as fleas and ticks, only spend a small portion of their lives on the host. They are very difficult to exterminate because both the host and the environment must be treated.

When treating dogs for external parasites, label instructions provided by the manufacturer should be followed closely. Most labels will warn that pregnant bitches and young puppies should not be treated with pesticides. Professional help may be sought from a veterinarian and from an expert, licensed exterminator.

External parasites that plague North American dogs include various forms of fleas, ticks, lice and mites. Each will be discussed individually.

FLEAS

Fleas are the most annoying parasite known to both dogs and dog owners. They spend little time on the dog and thus are extremely difficult to exterminate. Adult fleas jump onto a dog, take a blood meal and then promptly jump off again. If another dog is handy, the flea may jump onto the second dog, thus facilitating the communicability of this pest. If no other dog is handy, the adult flea will remain in the environment waiting for its next meal and laying eggs in the interim. The eggs laid by adult fleas may lie dormant for several months. Under ideal environmental conditions, larvae will emerge from the eggs in about three weeks. With time, the larvae will grow into adult fleas and repeat the entire cycle.

To disrupt the life cycle of the flea, both the host and the environment must be treated at intervals of three to four weeks. If the dog is treated and the environment is neglected, the dog will be reinfested by fleas left in the environment. Likewise, the environment will be recontaminated after treatment if the dog is neglected. Repeated treatments approximately one month apart will ensure that emerging larvae will be destroyed before they are able to mature and produce more eggs.

Several types of products have been marketed for flea control on the dog. Dips, shampoos, powders and sprays are the most common products of this type.

Dips are concentrated rinses that must be diluted before being applied to the dog. They should be applied to the entire dog to kill all fleas and should be left on the dog to enhance residual activity of the pesticide.

Most flea shampoos must be left on the sudsy dog for ten minutes before rinsing in order to kill fleas present on the dog. Since flea shampoos are ultimately rinsed off the dog, they have no residual effect.

Powders are sprinkled onto the dog and then combed through

the coat. Because they remain on the dog, they have some residual activity. Dogs with short coats, however, do not retain much of the powder. Powders can be inconvenient to use because they are messy. They are, however, usually considered safe for use on puppies.

Flea sprays must be applied to the entire dog in order to be effective. They can be difficult to use because most dogs do not like the procedure and are uncooperative during application. In addition, the dog's hair must be brushed against the grain while applying the spray. Many sprays contain a large percentage of alcohol, which can dry a dog's coat.

Many other products have been devised to control fleas on the dog. Flea collars are among the most popular. Traditional flea collars are impregnated with a pesticide. Often they simply encourage fleas to find refuge at the tail end of the dog rather than near the neck. Electronic flea collars have been touted as the latest, safest rage. Scientific studies have been unable to substantiate any merit for their use.

Caution must be exercised when treating any young puppy with pesticides, as puppies are extremely susceptible to poisoning. Many times the safest measure is to treat the environment and neglect treating the puppy until it is older. Flea powder may be placed under the bedding of crates or whelping boxes to control fleas. The powder should never contact the bitch's nipples or other sources of food for the puppies.

Pesticides are used to kill adult fleas both on the dog and in the environment. Many different pesticides are available for use in exterminating fleas. The reason that so many pesticides have been manufactured is that the flea is very versatile. It adapts rapidly. For this reason, pesticide rotation is recommended. That is, a different pesticide should be used each time the dog or environment is treated.

Three basic categories of pesticides are available to treat fleas: citrus-based, pyrethrin-based and those based on organophosphates. Citrus-based products are advocated as being "natural." Pyrethrins have proven to be relatively safe and may be used in combination with organophosphates, if necessary. Organophosphates, on the other hand, should not be combined with one another or a combined toxicity may result.

Many of these products have been microencapsulated. That is, they have been treated so that they are time-released to last in the environment for longer periods of time.

Flea eggs are resistant to pesticides. Therefore, frequent vacuuming is recommended. The vacuum will remove the eggs from the environment. Vacuum bags should be filled with moth balls or flea powder and discarded frequently to eliminate emerging larvae.

Methoprene (Precor) is an insect growth hormone regulator. It is not a pesticide and therefore does not kill adult fleas. Instead, methoprene effectively prevents flea larvae from maturing into adult fleas. Unfortunately it is destroyed by sunlight and is easily vacuumed away. Several other insect hormones have recently been formulated that may have a greater residual activity.

Citronella is a natural insect repellent that may have some effect in warding off fleas without actually killing them. Likewise, Avon Skin-So-Soft may have some repellent action. Many veterinary dermatologists advocate using one part of Avon Skin-So-Soft in four parts water as a mist to repel fleas.

Keep in mind that the flea war can be won only by fighting fleas both on the host and in the environment. Often each dog is not treated or the environment is neglected. All the dogs, the house, the kennel, the yard and even the van must be treated in order to eliminate fleas. Any household cats must be kept indoors or they will simply bring fleas home with them. Treatment must also be repeated at regular intervals in order to disrupt the flea's life cycle.

TICKS

Two kinds of hard ticks are commonly found on dogs in the United States. They are the American dog tick (*Dermacentor variabilis*) and the brown dog tick (*Rhipicephalus sanguineus*). *Ixodes dammini* is a tiny, soft tick that carries Lyme disease and may also infect dogs.

All ticks are blood-sucking parasites. Once a female tick is engorged with blood, she will drop off her host to lay her eggs. Those eggs will hatch into larvae that will climb onto various hosts to feed, dropping to the ground between feeding on each host. Larvae eventually mature into adult ticks. The adults climb onto a host to copulate and feed.

Because ticks are blood-sucking parasites, heavy infestations may cause an anemia in dogs. Because the ticks go through several hosts, they readily transmit blood-borne, contagious diseases between animals. Some of the diseases that they can transmit include

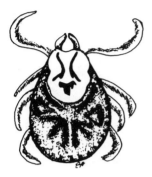

Hard Tick

Soft Tick

Biting Louse

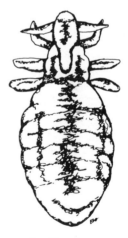

Sucking Louse

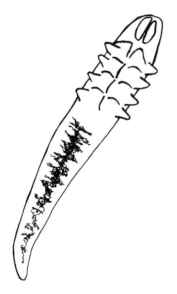

Demodectic Mite   Sarcoptic Mite

babesiosis, Rocky Mountain spotted fever, tularemia and Lyme disease.

If a few ticks are found on a dog, they may be extracted manually. To make sure that contagious diseases are not spread to humans, care should be taken not to handle ticks with bare hands. If many ticks are present, they should be eliminated with an appropriate dip. The premises should also be treated, especially if the brown dog tick is found. The brown dog tick is capable of infesting kennels. Dogs should be kept from reentering sylvan areas known to be infested with ticks.

LICE

Lice are classified by their feeding habits as either biting lice or sucking lice. Both types of lice may infest dogs, although neither type is seen commonly. The sucking louse ingests blood from its host and may cause an anemia in infested dogs. The biting louse lives on the scurf of the skin and may cause much irritation. Lice are spread rapidly by direct contact. They may be diagnosed by finding either adults or eggs on a microscopic examination of a skin scraping. Since their entire life cycle is spent on the host, lice are effectively treated with a variety of insecticidal dips.

MITES

Four types of mites may be found on dogs: *Otodectes, Cheyletiella, Sarcoptes* and *Demodex*.

Otodectic mites are more commonly referred to as ear mites. They spend their entire life cycle within the ear of their host. Both dogs and cats can act as hosts and can transmit ear mites to each other. Most affected pets have a dark brown, waxy discharge in their ears and scratch at the ears. Untreated pets eventually develop severe ear infections and may have a puslike discharge. Ear mites should be treated with a topical insecticide for the ears, and flea powder should be sprinkled around the ears to kill any stray ear mites. Any associated ear infection should be treated by a veterinarian.

Cheyletiella infestation is more commonly called walking dandruff because infected animals appear to have a severe case of dandruff. The dandruff is seen primarily along the back. Affected animals are not usually itchy. These mites may infest dogs, cats, rabbits, foxes and man. They may be diagnosed with a skin scraping. Since the entire life cycle is spent on the host, *Cheyletiella* may be effectively treated with a number of insecticidal dips. All contact animals must also be treated in order to eliminate the mites.

Scabies is an intensely itchy, highly contagious mange caused by the sarcoptic mite. Some dogs may harbor the mite without signs and other dogs may incubate the mite for as long as two months before showing signs. The mite is fairly host specific but may transiently infect other species, such as human beings and cats. Scabies mites are difficult to find on skin scrapings, and many cases are diagnosed on clinical signs. Fortunately, the mite spends its entire life cycle on the host. Since asymptomatic carriers exist, all contact animals should be treated. Paramite (Vet-Kem) is currently the only dip licensed for the treatment of scabies in dogs. Often, the dips must be repeated many times to effect a cure. A veterinarian should be consulted if scabies is suspected.

Small numbers of demodectic mange mites are found as normal inhabitants of healthy canine skin. Disease occurs when an individual dog has a faulty immune system and the mite multiplies unabated. Except for the transmission of mites to newborns from a bitch, demodectic mites are not contagious. Two forms of the disease exist. Generalized demodectic mange is believed to have a hereditary basis. Thus, the Academy of Veterinary Dermatology recommends neutering all dogs with generalized demodicosis. Dogs with localized *Demodex* may be treated with Mitaban (amitraz). Amitraz is the only dip licensed for use in treating *Demodex*. It is available only through veterinary prescription.

20

Understanding Diagnostic Tests

WHEN A VISIT to the veterinarian is warranted, a thorough history and physical examination may be all that is needed to identify and solve the problem. Sometimes, however, resolution requires more information than an accurate history and complete physical exam can yield. Ancillary diagnostic tests may be required.

The group of tests that a veterinarian chooses to use when investigating a particular problem is referred to as a minimum data base. This often consists of one or more of the following: a complete blood cell count with a differential, a chemistry screen, a fecal examination, a urine analysis and radiographs. It is important to understand what information each of these diagnostic tests may provide.

COMPLETE BLOOD CELL COUNT

A complete blood cell count (CBC) is measured from a sample of the patient's blood. Basically, it provides information regarding the concentration of both white blood cells (WBC) and red blood cells (RBC). Many bacterial infections cause the WBC to be markedly increased above normal values, while some viral infections cause the WBC to be markedly decreased. Parvovirus, for example, causes a drop in the concentration of WBC. Anemia is evidenced by a decrease in the concentration of RBC. Blood loss secondary to trauma or to blood-sucking parasites often causes an anemia.

The differential is usually an integral part of the CBC. It describes what kind of blood cells are present. Blood contains many different kinds of WBC. Neutrophils are a type of WBC that aids the body in fighting bacterial infections. Eosinophils are another type of WBC that aids the body in fighting parasites and allergic reactions. Normal red blood cells have no nuclei. The presence of nucleated RBC may indicate that a disease such as lead poisoning is present. Obviously, a wealth of information can be gained from a CBC and differential count.

CHEMISTRY SCREEN

A sample of the patient's blood is also used to obtain a chemistry screen. The specific contents of a chemistry screen will vary from one laboratory to another but will always consist of a panel of results. This panel frequently evaluates both kidney and liver function. It measures the levels of important blood components such as sugar (glucose), proteins (albumin and globulin) and electrolytes (sodium, potassium, calcium and phosphorus).

Two values on the typical chemistry screen will evaluate kidney function. They are creatinine and blood urea nitrogen. If the value for creatinine is markedly elevated above normal, significant kidney function has been lost. The blood urea nitrogen (BUN) is a better indicator of kidney function in puppies that are still growing. If the BUN is elevated in a sample from a puppy, significant kidney function has probably been lost. Kidney failure is most often noted in older dogs as a part of the aging process. It occasionally results from a congenital defect or a poisoning.

A number of values can be used to evaluate liver function. They typically include SGPT, bilirubin, SGOT and SAP. In general, the SGPT and bilirubin values are used to identify disease of the liver itself, while SGOT and SAP are used to identify an obstruction of the liver's outlet for bile. Typically, both the liver and its outlet are simultaneoously diseased and all four values will be elevated.

A multitude of diseases may cause liver failure, including cancer, poisons and infections.

High levels of blood glucose usually indicate diabetes, while low levels of blood glucose may result from many different causes. Most diabetic dogs have an insatiable thirst. Neurological signs such as weakness and seizures occur in many patients with a low blood sugar level.

Albumin and globulin, two different types of proteins, are often evaluated on a routine chemistry screen. Low albumin may be caused by many digestive, kidney and liver diseases. High globulin levels indicate a systemic infection and may coincide with a fever.

Several electrolyte values are provided on a chemistry screen. The most commonly evaluated electrolytes include sodium, potassium, calcium and phosphorus. Electrolyte values must be considered in relation to one another. Sodium and potassium levels, for example, are often inversely related. Patients with Cushing's disease may have a simultaneous increase in sodium and a decrease in potassium. Patients with Addison's disease may have a simultaneous decrease in sodium and an increase in potassium. Many other disease states will alter sodium and potassium levels. Each is evidenced by a variety of clinical symptoms.

Calcium and phosphorus levels are also often inversely related. Nutritional secondary hyperparathyroidism, for example, is caused by a dietary imbalance and is evidenced by an elevation of calcium with a concurrent depletion of phosphorus. Hypocalcemia secondary to reproductive diseases and hyperphosphatemia secondary to kidney failure may not, however, display this inverse relationship. As you can see, the interpretation of electrolyte values can be quite complicated and is best left in the hands of a competent veterinarian.

In special cases, the minimum data base may include other blood tests. For example, hypothyroidism, occult heartworm infections and bleeding disorders may be diagnosed through blood tests.

FECAL EXAMINATIONS

Fecal examinations are performed so routinely that their value is often underestimated. Fecal exams are a part of the minimum data base for any case of vomiting or diarrhea and for many other signs of disease.

URINE ANALYSIS

A urine analysis is often a part of a minimum data base. Urine samples may be collected by three different means. Most are collected as "midstream, free-catch samples"—in other words, urine is collected while the dog voids. Since the first few drops of urine will be contaminated by dirt and bacteria on the skin, samples should be caught in the middle of the stream. Urine may also be collected through a urinary catheter. Occasionally, urine is obtained through a technique called cystocentesis, in which a needle is inserted through the skin of the dog directly into the bladder.

The routine urine analysis consists of two parts. The first is referred to as a dipstick. A stick containing color-coded patches is saturated with urine. Color changes will indicate the acidity of the sample and whether or not there is any evidence of urinary tract bleeding, kidney disease, liver disease or diabetes.

The second part of a routine urine analysis is the sediment evaluation. A sample of urine is placed in a test tube and centrifuged so that any solid material will spin to the bottom of the tube. This solid material, or sediment, may contain RBC, WBC and crystals if a bladder infection is present. The sediment may contain casts if a serious kidney problem exists.

Urine samples should be collected into sterile containers, if possible. A culture and sensitivity test may be performed on a urine sample if it is collected in a sterile manner. The urine is first cultured on a medium so that any offending bacteria may grow. Then antibiotics are tested to see if they will kill the growing bacteria. Cultures and sensitivities are used to better treat recurrent bladder infections.

RADIOGRAPHS

Radiographs have become an integral part of the minimum data base for many signs of disease other than the obvious sign of lameness. Typically, two or three viewpoints are taken so that a three-dimensional image can be envisioned. When the chest is being evaluated, two radiographs are usually taken. In one, the dog is lying on its right side. This is called a right lateral view. In the other, the dog is lying on its chest. This is known as a dorsoventral view. Similarly, when the abdomen is being evaluated, two radiographs are usually taken. The only difference is that a ventrodorsal view is

216

usually substituted for the dorsolateral view. To obtain a ventro-dorsal view, the dog must be placed on its back.

These routine radiographs are often referred to as survey films. Many special techniques are available to aid survey films. In one technique, known as a pneumocystogram, air is injected into the bladder through a urinary catheter. Such a special study is valuable in identifying some bladder stones and tumors. Another special technique is the barium study. A mixture containing the chemical element barium is force-fed to the patient, whose digestive system is then radiographed. The barium appears white on a radiograph and will outline the digestive system. Barium studies are an invaluable aid in diagnosing intestinal obstructions.

Table 20-1
Complete Blood Count

	Normal	*Patient*		*Normal*	*Patient*
WBC × 1000	6–17		Lymphs × 1000	1–4.8	
Neuts × 1000	3–11.5		RBC × 1,000,000	5.5–8.5	
Bands × 1000	0–0.3		Hematocrit (%)	37–55	
Eos × 1000	0.1–1.2		Hemoglobin (g/dl)	12–18	
Basos × 1000	rare		Nucl. RBC's	rare	
Monos × 1000	0.1–1.4				

Table 20–2
Chemistry Screen

	*Normal**	*Patient*		*Normal**	*Patient*
Creatinine	0.6–1.8		SAP	10–115	
BUN	7–33		Glucose	60–140	
SGPT	15–55		Total protein	5–7.5**	
Bilirubin	0–1		Calcium	8–12	
SGOT	10–25				

*Normal values taken from a Du Pont Analyst benchtop chemistry system.
**Normal values taken from a standard refractometer.

Table 20-3
Urine Analysis

pH	RBC's
Blood	WBC's
Protein	Crystals
Bilirubin	Bacteria
Glucose	Casts
Ketones	Other
Specific gravity	

It is imperative to recognize the state of a dog's health when one works with numbers of animals. Attitude, activity level and overall appearance are all signposts to the experienced dog keeper— amateur or professional. *Mintzer*

This well-kept professional handler's kennel is managed with scrupulous hygiene in order to protect the health and safety of the dogs living there. Any kennel can be a breeding ground for contagious diseases if housekeeping and sanitation procedures are not strictly observed.

21

Recognizing Common Signs of Disease

KENNEL MANAGERS must be able to recognize rapidly any potential signs of disease in order to initiate prompt and effective care. In general, if a disease is recognized rapidly, treatment is more likely to be successful.

The kennel situation provides fertile ground for the rapid spread of contagious diseases. If one dog can be spotted as being ill before kennel mates begin showing signs of the same contagious disease, the kennel as a whole will benefit markedly.

A kennel manager must learn to recognize and record signs. This will enable him or her to provide a complete, thorough and accurate history to a veterinarian when he or she is called upon to perform a physical examination and gather a minimum data base. Common signs of disease include vomiting, diarrhea, coughing, polydipsia (increased thirst), dysuria (painful urination), lameness and pruritis (itchiness). Each of these signs will be discussed in depth so that important details can be noted by observant owners.

VOMITING

Vomiting is defined as the active expulsion of stomach contents. It is simply a sign of disease and not a definitive diagnosis. Vomiting should be distinguished from productive coughing and from regurgitation. With a productive cough, mucus is expelled. When a dog regurgitates, it expels food passively without heaving motions. Regurgitated food is often tubular in form.

The contents of the vomitus should be noted, as well as the frequency, duration and timing of the vomiting. The vomitus may contain foreign bodies (such as plants and toys), food or stomach juices, which are clear and yellow. Blood is occasionally present in the vomitus. Vomiting many times during a given day indicates an acute problem, while vomiting once a day over a period of time indicates a more chronic problem. The timing of the act of vomiting in relation to the time of feeding is important to note. Vomiting may occur immediately after or many hours after feeding. The former would indicate disease of the stomach, while the latter would indicate a disease of more distal parts of the digestive tract. Infectious causes of vomiting tend to bear no relation to the time food is eaten.

When a dog is vomiting, it should be watched closely so that its appetite and stool consistency can be monitored. The affected dog should also be closely watched to detect other signs of disease because vomiting may be the primary sign of diseases that affect body systems other than the digestive system. Vomiting may be a serious sign and should not be ignored.

The causes of vomiting in dogs are innumerable. Viral and intestinal parasitic infections commonly cause vomiting. Inflammatory diseases that may cause vomiting include pancreatitis and peritonitis. Pancreatitis, an inflammation of the pancreas, often occurs secondary to dietary indiscretion. It is seen most often in overweight, middle-aged bitches. Peritonitis is an inflammation of the abdominal lining. It may be caused by a ruptured bowel or a ruptured uterus. Mechanical obstruction due to the ingestion of foreign bodies usually causes severe, acute vomiting. Often, all food and water will be vomited. Obstruction requires immediate surgical correction.

Obstruction can also be caused by bloat, intussusception, herniated bowels or tumors. Bloat is a medical emergency that is caused by an accumulation of gas within the stomach. Intussusception is also an emergency. It is caused by hyperactivity of the intestinal muscle wall that causes one part of the intestine to telescope over another part of the intestine. Either the uterus or segments of bowel may herniate through rents in the body wall, most of which are found in the umbilicus or one of the inguinal canals. Drugs, toxins and metabolic diseases such as diabetes may also cause vomiting.

The minimum data base for most vomiting dogs consists of a fecal exam, a CBC, a chemistry screen and abdominal radiographs.

Symptomatic, home treatment is similar for both vomiting and diarrhea. The stomach should be rested for twenty-four hours by withholding food. If the vomiting has stopped, bland food can then be given. A mixture of hamburger and cooked white rice is an example of a bland diet. For each two-thirds cup of rice, one-third cup of hamburger is added. Small meals should be offered frequently for several days. If the vomiting does not resolve, a veterinarian should be consulted.

Veterinary care is indicated anytime that a vomiting dog is depressed, anorexic or unable to keep any food or water down. These additional signs may indicate an intestinal obstruction or perforation. Prompt veterinary care is needed for such diseases, as they present surgical emergencies.

DIARRHEA

Diarrhea is the production of abnormal stool. It is not a disease in and of itself. Rather, it is merely a sign of one of many possible underlying diseases.

Diarrhea is usually classified as being either small bowel or large bowel in origin. Diarrhea may also be classified as acute or chronic in nature. Small bowel diarrhea usually produces a large volume of stool to be passed. The small bowel is responsible for absorbing nutrients from food. Therefore, chronic small bowel diarrhea causes significant weight loss. Large bowel diarrhea is commonly referred to as colitis. It usually causes small volumes of soft stool to be defecated with an increased frequency. Frequently colitis is also evidence by mucoid, blood-tinged stools because the large bowel normally produces mucus to lubricate stools. Colitis may also cause straining.

Any dog with diarrhea should be monitored closely and leash walked, if necessary. The frequency of defecation, volume of stool produced with each defecation, color and odor of feces, the presence of any blood or mucus and any difficulty passing stools should be recorded.

Historically, it is also important to note the age and breed of any dog with diarrhea. Classically, young dogs are more likely to acquire diarrhea due to infections, parasites and dietary indiscretions; older dogs are more likely to develop cancer. German Shepherd Dogs may develop a condition know as pancreatic enzyme insufficiency. In this condition, the pancreas does not produce digestive enzymes; therefore, the dog cannot digest food. Chronic, small bowel diarrhea and emaciation result. Boxers, on the other hand, are likely to develop a condition known as idiopathic colitis. The cause of this condition is unknown. Affected dogs have large bowel diarrhea.

Dietary changes and indiscretions are important historical notations. They may explain many simple cases of diarrhea. It is important to note whether or not any possibility exists for garbage ingestion or poisoning.

There are innumerable causes of diarrhea in dogs. Most cases of diarrhea go undiagnosed. The minimum data base for diarrhea always includes a fecal examination. Young dogs suspected of a viral diarrhea should also have a CBC performed. Older dogs should have a chemistry screen done. Any dog suspected of consuming a foreign body should have radiographs taken; a barium study may be necessary to identify some foreign bodies.

Symptomatic, home treatment may be undertaken for simple cases of diarrhea. A simple case of diarrhea can be defined as one in which the affected dog remains bright and alert, continues to eat well and is not vomiting. Symptomatic treatment of diarrhea includes removing food for twenty-four hours. When food is reintroduced, it should be bland (see Vomiting). Stools should begin to re-form in two to three days. At that time it will be safe to begin gradually adding dog food to the diet. The transition back to a normal diet should take place over two to three days. Any dog that does not respond or relapses should be examined by a veterinarian.

COUGHING

Coughing is a warning that respiratory disease exists. Although coughing has a protective function, excessive coughing can itself be harmful.

Coughs are usually described as either nonproductive or productive. Nonproductive coughs are dry and harsh. With productive coughs, mucus is expelled. Productive coughing is often confused with vomiting.

Respiratory disease may be defined as either "upper" or "lower." Upper respiratory disease is limited to the nose, throat and major airways. Lower respiratory disease involves the lungs themselves and is often quite serious. Respiratory disease may be secondary to disease of another organ system. For example, some heart diseases eventually cause respiratory disease and result in coughing.

Because the list of possible diseases that may cause coughing is endless, an accurate history is invaluable. The breed, age and sex of a coughing dog are important to note. Toy and brachycephalic breeds of dogs are predisposed to obstructive upper airway diseases. An overlong soft palate and stenotic nares (small nostrils) are two common causes of obstructive disease. Small breeds commonly develop heart valve disease with age, while giant breeds commonly develop cardiomyopathy with age. Boxers are prone to develop tumors within the chest. Younger dogs are more likely to be exposed to respiratory infections. Older, unspayed female dogs may develop breast cancer, which often spreads to the lungs.

Environmental history is also important to note. Contagious diseases such as kennel cough are acquired through exposure to other dogs, usually at dog shows or boarding kennels. A sick dog's vaccination history and both fecal and heartworm status are important to note so that certain infectious and parasitic diseases may be ruled out of the list of possible causes.

All coughing dogs should be examined by a veterinarian, even if kennel cough is strongly suspected. Although ancillary tests may not be necessary, affected dogs should be treated with appropriate antibiotics and cough suppressants. If another disease is suspected, the minimum data base may include a CBC, a fecal examination, heartworm tests and chest radiographs.

POLYDIPSIA

"Polydipsia" is the medical term for excessive thirst. It is often difficult to ascertain just when thirst is excessive, because several environmental factors will influence water consumption. One factor is environmental temperature. Dogs simply tend to drink more in warm weather. Diet is another factor. Dogs fed dry food consume more water than dogs fed canned food. Additionally, some foods contain more salt than other foods and hence encourage water consumption. Certain drugs are known to consistently cause polydipsia and include sulfa-type antibiotics and corticosteroids.

Increased thirst may be a sign of a serious underlying disease. Common, serious causes of polydipsia include diabetes, pyometritis, liver failure, kidney failure and Cushing's disease. Fever sometimes causes polydipsia, as can protracted digestive system diseases. Vomiting in combination with diarrhea may cause a dog to drink more in order to keep up with water lost through the digestive system.

A general rule of thumb can help to define normal thirst. Most adult dogs will drink about one cup of water for each ten pounds of body weight per day. Puppies normally consume twice as much water as adults. Monitoring thirst in an individual dog requires some effort in multiple dog households, if necessary by isolating that individual in an individual run or crate, in order to record daily water intake. If this is not possible, all household water should be removed and water should be offered individually as often as possible. As much water as the suspect dog will drink should be offered at least four times daily. Polydipsic dogs should never be deprived of water without direct veterinary supervision.

Most dogs with polydipsia also have polyuria, an increased volume of urine production. Indoor dogs may have urinary accidents as a result.

A CBC, chemistry screen and urine analysis comprise the minimum data base for any dog with polydipsia. Home treatment should not be attempted unless the change in thirst can be directly attributed to a dietary cause.

DYSURIA

Dysuria is defined as "painful urination." Owners may notice that an affected dog is straining to urinate, has blood in the urine or is urinating with an increased frequency.

Causes of dysuria include bladder infections with or without concomitant bladder stones, tumors of the urinary tract usually involving the bladder or the prostate gland and bleeding disorders such as von Willebrand's disease.

224

Dogs presenting to a veterinarian for a first episode of dysuria are frequently placed on antibiotics. If the affected dog does not improve or if dysuria recurs, ancillary tests are needed. The minimum data base will include a CBC and a urine analysis. Occasionally a culture and sensitivity of a urine sample and radiographs of the abdomen are indicated. If bladder stones are discovered, surgery will probably be needed.

There is no home treatment for dysuria.

LAMENESS

Lameness is a sign that there is a problem with one or more limbs. The problem may involve the nervous system, bone or associated soft tissues, such as muscles or ligaments.

Lameness may be termed as either weight-bearing or non-weight-bearing. In general the more serious injuries produce a totally nonweight-bearing lameness in which the affected dog holds the limb flexed off the ground. Almost all dogs with broken bones will be unable to bear weight on the affected leg. Such dogs are often described as "three-legged lame." Lameness may also be described as intermittent, continuous or shifting. Intermittent lameness comes and goes; continuous lameness does not. Shifting lameness may alternate from one leg to another and back again.

Location alone can be a good clue as to the precise cause of a lameness. The wrist, the elbow and the shoulder are common sites for forelimb lamenesses. The wrist is a common site for lacerations, bone cancer and pounding injuries. The elbow is subject to both dysplasia and fractures. The shoulder is a common site for osteochrondrosis dessicans and tumors.

The knee and the hip are common sites for hind limb lamenesses. The knee is subject to congenital deformities of the joint and is also subject to cruciate ligament injuries. The hip may be affected with either Legg-Calve-Perthes' disease or hip dysplasia. Both of these hip deformities predispose dogs to total luxation of the hip joint.

General causes of lameness can be classified as fractures, soft tissue injuries, arthritic conditions, spinal diseases and metabolic abnormalities. Again, history is very important in determining the cause and predicting the prognosis of a lameness.

Fractures usually occur secondary to a known injury and cause

225

a sudden onset of nonweight-bearing, continuous lameness. Fractures must be treated by a veterinarian.

Soft tissue wounds are usually obvious and should be cleansed thoroughly. Since wounds can vary in severity, the degree and kind of lameness resulting can also vary in degree. Lameness may be delayed for some time after an injury if the wound causes a bone infection to result. Therefore, if a wound appears to be extensive, it should be examined by a veterinarian.

Arthritis may develop secondarily to an injury or to a congenital defect such as hip dysplasia. Signs of arthritis usually develop slowly and progressively. With time, arthritic animals will be worst after resting and will appear to warm out of the pain with exercise. Cold, damp conditions may exacerbate signs. Arthritis may be one component of a systemic disease such as lupus or Lyme disease, and other signs of disease may also be present.

Several spinal diseases commonly cause lameness. They include intervertebral disk disease, wobbler syndrome and trauma. Cervical disk disease usually causes neck pain, while thoracolumbar disk disease results in varying degrees of hind limb weakness. Disk disease is usually seen in short-legged, long-backed breeds of dogs as young adults. Wobbler syndrome is often seen in Dobermans and Great Danes. Since the bones of the neck are malformed, the spinal cord is adversely affected. Most dogs with wobbler syndrome are uncoordinated, especially with regard to their hind limbs. Many automobile accidents result in spinal injury. Particular signs will depend upon which part of the spine is damaged and to what degree.

Age and breed are important factors to take note of when diagnosing metabolic causes of lamenesses. Young dogs of certain breeds are predisposed to develop metabolic causes of lameness, such as panosteitis and hypertrophic osteodystrophy. Panosteitis is often seen in young German Shepherds. It causes an intermittent, shifting, weight-bearing lameness in both fore and hind legs. Hypertrophic osteodystrophy is a disease of growing puppies that causes swelling of the wrist and sometimes the hocks. Pain is intermittent and may be accompanied by fever. Affected puppies are often reluctant to even stand or move. No exact cause or treatment is known for these metabolic bone disorders.

The minimum data base for any lameness usually includes radiographs.

Home treatment is often limited to cage rest and exercise re-

A dog's age and its breed are factors to consider in diagnosing metabolic causes of lameness. Different breeds will vary in predispositions to a variety of conditions.

striction. The use of aspirin, under veterinary supervision, may be the recommended course to treat some cases of arthritis.

PRURITIS

Pruritis is an unpleasant skin sensation that causes dogs to scratch at themselves. In many kennel situations the pruritic dog is not noted to scratch at itself. Rather, the dog appears to have self-induced, traumatic skin lesions that are caused by biting, rubbing, licking and/or scratching.

It is important to watch an affected dog to see that it is truly pruritic and to be certain that the visible skin lesions are indeed secondary to self-induced trauma. Some skin diseases, such as hypothyroidism, are typically nonpruritic. It is also important to note whether the pruritis is seasonal. If it is seasonal, an allergy may be suspected. An observation should be made regarding which portions of the body are affected. The distribution of lesions will often hint at the cause. For example, scabies classically affects the ears and the elbows, while flea allergies typically affect the back and the thighs.

The most common causes of pruritis are parasitic (fleas and scabies) and allergic (fleas, food and inhalants). Healthy skin is, however, dependent on all other body systems. Thus, diseases that affect other organ systems may present with skin problems.

No minimum data base is usually required. If ancillary tests are required, they usually include a skin scraping to search for mites, a culture for ringworm and skin testing for allergies. Occasionally a skin biopsy will provide a diagnosis.

Home treatment includes stringent parasite control and routine grooming.

Bibliography

Braund, K.G. *Clinical Syndromes in Veterinary Neurology*. Baltimore: Williams and Wilkens, 1986.

Clark, R.D., and J.R. Stainer (eds.). *Medical & Genetic Aspects of Purebred Dogs*. Edwardsville, Kan.: Veterinary Medical Publishing Co., 1983.

Ettinger, S.J. *Textbook of Veterinary Internal Medicine*. 2nd ed. Philadelphia: W.B. Saunders, 1983.

Evans, H.E., and G.C. Christensen (eds.). *Miller's Anatomy of the Dog*. Philadelphia: W.B. Saunders, 1979.

Feldman, B.F. (ed.). "Hemostasis," in *Veterinary Clinics of North America*, vol. 18, no. 1. Philadelphia: W.B. Saunders, 1988.

Fenner, W.R. *Quick Reference to Veterinary Medicine*. Philadelphia: Lippincott, 1982.

Grieve, R.B. (ed.). "Parasitic Infections," in *Veterinary Clinics of North America*, vol. 17, no. 6. Philadelphia: W.B. Saunders, 1987.

Johnston, S.D. *Canine Reproduction*. Minneapolis: University of Minnesota, 1989.

Kealy, J.K. *Diagnostic Radiology of the Dog and Cat*. Philadelphia: W.B. Saunders, 1979.

Kirk, R.W. and S.I. Bistner. *Handbook of Veterinary Procedures and Emergency Treatment*. 3rd ed. Philadelphia: W.B. Saunders, 1981.

Lawler, D.F., and E.D. Colby (eds.). "Pediatrics," in *Veterinary Clinics of North America*, vol. 17, no. 3. Philadelphia: W.B. Saunders, 1987.

Lewis, L.D., M.L. Morris and M.S. Hand. *Small Animal Clinical Nutrition.* 3rd ed. Topeka: Mark Morris Associates, 1987.

Mosier, J.E. (ed.). "Symposium on Canine Pediatrics," in *Veterinary Clinics of North America*, vol. 8, no. 1. Philadelphia: W.B. Saunders, 1978.

Muller, G.H., R.W. Kirk and D.W. Scott: *Small Animal Dermatology.* 3rd ed. Philadelphia: W.B. Saunders, 1983.

Ralston Purina Co. *Nutrition & Management of Dogs and Cats.* 2nd ed. St. Louis: Ralston Purina Co., 1981.

Severin, G.A. *Veterinary Opthalmology Notes.* Fort Collins: Colorado State University, 1976.

Slatter, D.H. *Textbook of Small Animal Surgery.* Philadelphia: W.B. Saunders, 1984.

Weber, A.J. (publ.). *Veterinary Pharmaceuticals and Biologicals.* Lenexa, Kans.: Veterinary Medicine Publishing Company, 1986.